It is Well

For Teresa,

It is Well

A Study of Motherhood in Times of Crisis

I hope you'll be blessed by our stories. Love, Julie

Julie Christiansen

It is Well

It is Well

Other Titles by Julie Christiansen

Top Ten Lists to Live By

Anger Solutions: Proven Strategies for Effectively Resolving Anger and Taking Control of Your Emotions (Also available in audiobook and E-Book format)

Getting Past Your Past (Audio CD & Workbook)

When the Last Straw Falls: 30 Ways to Keep Stress from Breaking Your Back

Bullying is Not a Game: A Parents' Survival Guide

Anger Solutions by the Book: Biblical Principles for Resolving Anger

Anger Solutions by the Book Study Guide

It is Well

Leverage U Press
It is Well: A Study of Motherhood in Times of Crisis
©2019 by Leverage U & Julie Christiansen

LEVERAGE U

Requests for information should be addressed to: Leverage U
Julie Christiansen
73 Royal Manor Drive
St. Catharines, ON
L2M4L2
www.angersolution.com

All rights reserved. No part of this publication may be reproduced, stored in a retrieval system, or transmitted in any form or by any means – electronic, mechanical, photocopy, recording, or any other – except for brief quotations, without the prior written expressed permission of the publisher.

Printed in Canada.
Scripture quotations are from the King James Version of the Bible unless otherwise indicated. © 1973 by Word Aflame Press.

Christiansen, Julie A., 1968-
It is Well: A Study of Motherhood in Times of Crisis / Julie A. Christiansen
ISBN 13: 978-0979634-5-1

It is Well

A Study of Motherhood in Times of Crisis

Julie Christiansen

It is Well

It is Well

Contents

Introduction

Part One: Bitter

1. Poor Little Rich Girl
2. Bitter Can be Palatable
3. When Faith Dies
4. Bitter Waters
5. A Bitter Taste in Her Mouth
6. Making Bitter Better

Part Two: Better

7. 99 Bottles of Oil on the Wall
8. Bounty Borne of Gratitude
9. From Better to Blessed
10. Lord, Give Me Patience!

Part Three: Blessed

11. Don't Lie to Me!
12. Hannah's Song
13. When Crisis Comes

It is Well

14. When Your Daughter is Violated
15. When Your Son is in a Coma
16. When Your Child's Future is at Stake
17. Choices, Choices

References and Permissions

Acknowledgements

It is Well

Introduction

Your Imagination is Their Only Voice

Genesis chapter 4 tells the story of Cain and Abel. Cain, the firstborn of Adam and Eve, was a farmer, but Abel the younger brother, was a shepherd. We learn that Cain killed his brother out of jealousy, and for that vile act he was cast out from his family, cursed by God to be a vagrant and a fugitive for the rest of his days. We know that he found a family, married and had children. We also know that when Adam was one hundred and thirty years old, he and Eve conceived another child and she named him Seth, "For God, said she, hath appointed me another seed instead of Abel, whom Cain slew" (Genesis 4 v 25).

It is Well

What we do not know, because it is not recorded, is how Eve responded to the knowledge that one of her sons killed the other. We can imagine, but we cannot know for certain, how her heart must have broken when she saw the effect of sin in the world. What she must have thought when she realized that had she and Adam not partaken of the forbidden fruit, that both of her boys would still be alive and well. How she must have wept, cried, travailed and grieved for her children forever lost to her! Once her new baby was born, did she despair over fear of her son's future?

We do not know how long her time of grief persisted, or how long before she was convinced that she was deserving of having another child, Did she spend her days and nights overcome with anxiety that something else might happen that would take this new baby away from her too? Was she an overprotective mom, hovering around her son Seth, never allowing him to spread his wings and fulfill his potential out of fear that he too would be ripped away from her?

When Jochebed set her son adrift in a basket only to see him float directly into the arms of Pharaoh's daughter (Exodus 2 v 3-6), what kind of internal strength would she have needed to allow him to be taken into that household? Despite God's provision, essentially bringing her son back to her to be nursed until he was weaned, she must have worried about what was happening under Pharoah's roof and how her son was being indoctrinated into Egyptian tradition.

When Moses committed murder and ran from Egypt, disappearing into the wilderness, what did his mother think? How did she respond? When Moses returned to Egypt 40 years after his abrupt departure, was she still alive to see how God had transformed him? Did she die not knowing what her son would become, or how he would be mightily used of God to save a nation?
We are told Moses's story, but we know very little of his mother except that her great faith

It is Well

inspired her to do whatever was necessary to save his life in his early years. Whatever pain, grief, sorrow, regret, or other emotions she might have experienced while watching her son grow and develop from a distance, we will never know.

Many people give Bathsheba a "bad rap". After all, the woman was out bathing on her roof where anyone could see! (2 Samuel 11 v 2). When the king called for her, she went. *She must have been a loose woman!* Then again, the traditions of the still young Hebrew nation were not as they are now. When the king called, she had no choice but to answer. It is most likely that she feared for her life. Perhaps she thought, if I do not do what the king commands, he may have my husband killed in battle. Maybe she was so naïve that she thought the king would not have defiled her.

Can you imagine the guilt and shame she carried, knowing that she had betrayed her husband by engaging in adultery with the king? Have you ever wondered how terrified

It is Well

and alone she must have felt when she realized that she was pregnant? How long did she agonize over what to do about the baby before she sent word to the king to let him know she was with child? Who did she confide in? Who could she trust? Think about the emotional struggle she must have experienced during that time of her life.

As if being married to a military officer and being pregnant with the king's child wasn't enough, more crisis and tragedy was set to befall Bathsheba. Once the king set his final plan in motion to get rid of Uriah so that he could lawfully have his wife, how did Bathsheba respond? Imagine you were ordered to have a one-night-stand with the most powerful man in your country. You agree, knowing it is wrong, but you cannot see any way out that will end well. Then, you learn you are pregnant, and agonize over whether you should tell the king. Will he care? What might he do? Imagine you are dealing with all this alone, too afraid to trust anyone lest they judge you publicly for what you did in secret. Would they even believe you if you told them that the king of Israel got you pregnant? Not likely.

After struggling with all this alone, you learn that your husband has died a suspicious death on the battle field. Why would all the other soldiers retreat so that he and only he would be dealt a killing blow? Surely, this couldn't be coincidence... could it? You are grieving the premature death of your husband, and then you get a message from the palace saying the king has decided to make an honest woman of you (2 Samuel 11 v 26-27). Imagine it!

Put yourself in this poor woman's shoes. Do you honestly believe that all she felt at that moment was relief? Or was she conflicted, torn between emotions of grief for her loss, anger at the king for killing her husband, guilt and shame for her own part in this unfortunate turn of events? Do you think she went to the king willingly or reluctantly? We will never know, as the story was not told from Bathsheba's perspective.

Lastly, Bathsheba gives birth to her baby – a child borne of selfishness, sin and sorrow, the consequence of her and the king's mistakes. Then the child dies. Indulge me, dear reader, as I invite you to walk your imagination down this road with Bathsheba for a few moments. Did she grieve? For how long? We know what king David did – he wept and prayed over the child while it yet lived. He fasted and made supplication for the child. But when the child died, he got up, put on his robes, and went about the business of running the kingdom (2 Samuel 12 v 19-23).

Moms… would you be able to understand this response from your husbands? Would you do the same, or would you have a host of emotional detritus to wade through before you might feel whole again? Do you think that Bathsheba might have resented the king, her husband not by choice but by force, for having what to most mothers would appear to be a very calloused response to the death of her child? Do you think her life in the palace was all perfume and roses? I would suggest you think again. We can only imagine what

It is Well

Bathsheba may have suffered during that dark time of her life. Throughout this entire ordeal, as it is recorded in the Bible, Bathsheba's voice remains silent.

I think of other notable mothers in the Bible who suffered great tragedy related to their children. Imagine Mary's grief when Jesus died. Not one word is spoken of her agony. Was she hopeful? Did she know he would rise again? Did she, as she had done in her youth, hide the knowledge of this in her heart? Was she at peace? We cannot know. What of Elizabeth when John the Baptist was beheaded… but wait, she and Zachariah had their son in their old age. Was she even still alive when he was killed? Did she live to see the promises of God fulfilled in her son's life? We don't know.

There are so many women whose voices remain silent through the courses of history. Our imaginations combined with our own personal experiences as parents may be their only voice.

It is Well

The Mothers Whose Stories are Told
I believe that the women whose stories are recorded in the Bible have a purpose and a lesson beyond the obvious ones learned through the MAIN EVENT, which is always a demonstration of the providence and mercy of God. There is more to be learned through examination of the characters of the women in question.

I believe that as mothers, it is our destiny to face tragedy or crisis of some kind. There is no rule book that says mothers must outlive their children, or that a young mother will not lose a spouse in the early years of a marriage. There is no law that declares that motherhood is a bed of roses – in fact, where there are roses, there must be thorns. Along with the sweet comes the salty, the sour or the bitter. While we would love to avoid crises and tragedies, that is not our lot. The rain falls on the just and the unjust. Just because we moms birthed a watermelon sized human, enduring all the pain, discomfort and humiliation that often accompanies giving birth, it doesn't exempt us from worrying,

It is Well

agonizing, and grieving over our children when things go wrong throughout our motherhood journey. In fact, I believe it guarantees that we will experience great anguish as we walk with our children through times of great trial.

In my most recent season of crisis, it was the voices of other mothers, dear women of like precious faith, who spoke into my life, gave me advice, instilled hope, prayed for me and my family, and held me up when I could not stand on my own. The thing was this: while I was walking through fire with my family, I didn't search the Word to see what other mothers did when they were faced with what felt like impending doom. I was drawn instead to the psalms, those songs of David that reminded me that when my heart was overwhelmed, I could go to the rock that is higher than I. I modeled his unfailing trust in God. His cries for mercy spoke to me and I echoed those out to my God. Never once, I am embarrassed to say, did I dig deeper into the Word to see what the mothers of ancient days did or how they coped with their crises. Truth is, I was in crisis management mode. You know what this means, putting out fires, regulating the mood in the house, running to doctor's appointments, moderating conflicts, seeking advice, talking to lawyers, hospital visits, urgent prayers… there is no time for in-depth Bible study when your world is falling apart around you.

Instead, I did what I could. I went to the Psalms. I sang them. I cried them. I quoted them. I walked through the halls of my house, went into every room and prayed the Word over my children and my husband. I wept in secret. I pulled up my big girl panties and went to work, often talking with and counselling moms who were going through situations eerily like my own. Sometimes I had to stay home because I just could not handle hearing another mother's story while trying to live through my own season of chaos. I relied heavily on my husband, but also on church leadership and a community of mothers who had already journeyed down that lonely road of tragedy, pain, and heart-wrenching concern for their children.

It is Well

In retrospect, I wish that I had paid attention to the characters of the women to whom I will introduce you in this book. I have learned so much from examining their lives, their challenges, and the ways in which they responded. Whether in good times or bad, I had always been conscious of the fact that I could not allow myself to become bitter when life treated me unkind. I did not want the weeds of life to choke out the beautiful garden that God was and is making of my life. But I don't just want to be better; I want to be BLESSED. Don't you?

The purpose of this book is to introduce you to several women whose stories, although brief, are more than simple footnotes in the pages of Bible history. They are all moms who experienced some type of tragedy or crisis related to their children. You may think of those moms that have already been mentioned, but as I said, we study their stories often, but they are only in the periphery… we do not know much of what they felt, nor do we know how they responded to their family crises.

It is Well

The women you will meet here may not have had their names mentioned, but their voices ring out loudly and clearly. Listen closely. They have something to say. The message they have for you may change the way you approach crisis – and if that happens, then their stories would have fulfilled their purpose.

In addition to the stories from matriarchs of old, you will hear three tales from mothers of modern times including myself, sharing our stories of tragedy, crisis, grief, and recovery. It is my prayer for you that those trials that have become our testimonies will encourage and uplift you as you go through your own season of crisis.

It is Well

It is Well

PART ONE

Bitter

It is Well

It is Well

1

Poor Little Rich Girl

Mrs. Job flitted about her estate ordering the servants about with a dismissive air. She had a good life. Her husband was a good and honorable man. Well respected. A little too pious and honorable for her liking, but what did that matter? He was RICH!

She had given him seven sons and three daughters, guaranteeing both that their property and goods would stay in the family for at least another generation, and that there would be someone to take care of her in her old age. Her life was set.

Then suddenly tragedy struck, and in a big way. A messenger showed up at the house, the bearer of bad news. "The oxen were plowing and the donkeys feeding beside them, when the Sabeans raided them and took them away – indeed they have killed the servants with the edge of the sword, and I alone have escaped to tell you!" (Job 1 v 14)

It is Well

Another servant stumbled through the door, his head bloodied from a blow. "The Chaldeans formed three bands, raided the camels and stole them and killed the servants – I am the only one who survived!"

Yet another servant fell through the door, heavy with grief. Your sons and daughters were at your eldest son's house having dinner, and a tornado swept down and collapsed the house – they are all dead, and the servants too! I am so sorry! I am the only one who made it out."

In that moment, Mrs. Job's heart crumbled into a million pieces. She couldn't see beyond her pain – couldn't process her grief; that is why she never heard Job say, "The Lord gives and takes away, blessed be His name".

Weeks later, Job got sick… really sick. He was covered in boils and was too weak, or perhaps too depressed to even worry about seeing a doctor. Mrs. Job was still too entrenched in her own sorrow to take care of him. Frankly, his piety and trust in his unseen God had been getting on her nerves. Everything he said that was meant to be a comfort just grated on her further. *Her children were gone!* Her wealth and status were gone. Her possessions were gone. Her future security was gone. Everything was gone except her goody-two-shoes husband.

Finally, one day she found him where he had been for several days, sitting outside in a heap of ashes. She watched in disgust while he tried to burst his boils on his own with a broken piece of pottery, and suddenly her temper snapped. "Why on earth would you still hold fast to this integrity of yours? Where has it gotten you? Why don't you just curse God and die?" (Job 2 v 9)

I don't know about you, but every time I have heard a sermon or Bible study preached from this passage of scripture, I have asked myself, *"What kind of woman says this to her husband?"* Honestly. What kind of a shrew would you have to be to say such a horrible thing to the man you claim to love?

It is Well

Before we explore what might have motivated her to respond to her grief and pain in such a calloused way, let us first acknowledge the depth and breadth of Mrs. Job's loss. Can you imagine the depth of her grief? Step into her shoes for a moment and ask yourself, "how would I respond if in one fell swoop, I lost my wealth, my retirement plan, AND all my children?" Think of it! Ten of your babies. Ten human beings that you carried in your womb, laboured over and brought into the world. Ten souls that you nursed and cared and nurtured until they came of age. All those sleepless nights, the colic, the croup, the ear infections, scraped knees, broken limbs, all the "mom" worries times ten. All that love, all that time invested into what was for all intents and purposes, her legacy. To have all that wiped out in one fell swoop!

Yet, we have no record of her being bowed in grief. There is no telling of women from the community coming to her home to support her in her time of tremendous loss. We don't even know what it must have been like for her and her husband to bury all their children on the same day. I can only imagine the devastation of spirit she must have experienced. It would not surprise me if her heart literally felt as though it had been torn in ten.

Having acknowledged Mrs. Job's intense and unfathomable grief, I am still prompted to wonder how and why she came to turn on her husband in such a violent and hateful way. As a psychotherapist and someone who has always taken an interest in personality profiling, here is what I came up with.

Imagine a spoiled, self-indulgent, immature woman, whose interest is more in her material goods and her status in the community than it is in her relationship with her husband. She has lots of kids and a rich, kind husband, so for her, life is set. She can lounge around the house, go for mani-pedis, dote on her future grandchildren when they come around, and enjoy the easy life. Who cares if her husband is overzealous in his faith? No big deal. What does she care, so long as he keeps the money coming in?

It is Well

In my mind, when I picture Mrs. Job, I think: "Real Housewives of Ancient Days". I see her as a spoiled, self-indulgent "poor little rich girl" who lacked the empathy to care for others in their distress. Surely, she was attuned to her own grief and pain; however, I believe she lacked the ability to feel for those around her who might also be suffering – like her husband, Job. Otherwise, I can't fathom the motivation for that wicked, hurtful statement. I truly believe that by the time Mrs. Job came down to telling her husband just to die and get it over with, she was drowning in her own grief, angry that everything they had worked for was gone. That selfish, spoiled part of her may well have been thinking that if Job would just die, perhaps she could find another husband and maybe regain some of what she lost.

Perhaps that is just my cynical brain over-dramatizing the story. I believe Mrs. Job's challenge is that she did not share her husband's faith, nor did she have the emotional capacity to express her grief in healthy ways. Rather, she bottled it, allowing resentment and bitterness to fill her heart and taking hold until she could no longer stand the sight of her husband.

Had Mrs. Job shared in Job's faith, they would have together blessed the name of the Lord, and she might have been more accepting of their loss. That is not to say she would not have grieved her children; but she would have done so differently. Had she nurtured a different temperament and a more empathetic heart, she might have noticed that she was not the only one suffering.

While Job was able to say with confidence, "I know my redeemer lives" (Job 19:25), Mrs. Job had no such confidence. She was unable to reconcile Job's apparent peace during his loss because she did not know the peace-giver. She might have stepped up to defend her husband when she heard Job's "frenemies" blaming him for everything that had happened. Had she trusted in God the way that Job did, she might have had an inkling that their trial was not about her at all! Finally, she might have harboured hope in

It is Well

her God that He could restore what they had lost, even their family.

2
Bitter can be palatable

At the end of the book of Job, God indeed restored to him everything he had lost and then some. Even in this restoration, there was no mention of Mrs. Job. One can assume that she was the mother of the seven sons and three daughters with whom he was blessed, but we cannot know for certain.

The story reads as follows:

Job 41 v 10-17 *And the LORD turned the captivity of Job, when he prayed for his friends: also, the LORD gave Job twice as much as he had before. Then came there unto him all his brethren, and all his sisters, and all they that had been of his acquaintance before, and did eat bread with him in his house: and they bemoaned him, and comforted him over all the evil that the LORD had brought upon him: every man also gave him a piece of* money, and every one an earring of gold. So, the LORD blessed the latter end of Job more than his beginning: for he had fourteen thousand sheep, and six thousand camels, and a thousand yoke of oxen, and a thousand she asses. He had also seven sons and three daughters. And he called the name of the first, Jemima; and the name of the second, Kezia; and the name of the third, Kerenhappuch.

And in all the land were no women found so fair as the daughters of Job: and their father gave them inheritance among their brethren. After this lived Job an hundred and forty years, and saw his sons, and his sons' sons, even four generations. So, Job died being old and full of days.

The benefits of bitter
When you think of cooking with bitter foods, you might cringe at the thought. However, grapefruit, kale, broccoli, cabbage, even dark chocolate have qualities that are desirable such as strong anti-oxidant properties or cancer fighting properties. While bitterness is not something we enjoy, it may be essential

for our growth and development. Fat, sugar and salt are additives that can help mitigate the bitter flavour of foods.

After studying the passage in the book of Job, where his family and his wealth were restored, I have come to believe that God gave Job his three daughters to temper the bitter aftertaste of his time in the fire. I find it interesting too that the names of Job's daughters are mentioned, yet for all the times she is mentioned, his wife remains nameless.

Peace and Prosperity: Their first daughter mentioned was named Jemima, which means "dove" – a symbol of peace or the providence of God. The providence of God has oft been referred to in scripture of "fatness" – a reference to being in plenty. In Pharoah's dreams, the fat cows were interpreted by Joseph to represent a time of plenty or blessing. The skinny cows represented a time of famine and drought. Fat is a flavour enhancer. None of us is too excited to eat the "fat-free" version of any type of food. We just know that it won't be as flavourful as the stuff cooked in butter or olive oil, or bacon fat. The human body needs fat to survive. It helps to preserve heat, it is an alternate energy source, and without healthy fats, the brain would shrivel up and cease to function to its potential. If "fat" represents flavour enhancement, wealth and provision, Jemima is an apt name for that first daughter, one that represents the blessings of God having been restored in Job's life.

We do not know exactly how long Job's ordeal lasted for certain. We know that he lost everything in one day. We know then that he grew ill and was so for an undefined time. We also know that his three friends made plans, and then each travelled from their own homes to meet up at Job's to "comfort" him. Once they arrived there, they sat with him in silence for an entire week, out of acknowledgement of his great grief. We do not know how many days the following discourse lasted, but they were there for a while.

Where was Mrs. Job all this time? Was she listening to the debate between Job and his

It is Well

friends? Was she off somewhere feeling sorry for herself? Was she making sure they had food and drink, or did she abandon them to their own devices? We have some insight into her state in Job 19 v 14 to 17 (NASB): *"My relatives have failed, and my intimate friends have forgotten me. Those who live in my house and my maids consider me a stranger. I am a foreigner in their sight. I call to my servant, but he does not answer; I must implore him with my mouth. My breath is offensive to my wife, and I am loathsome to my own brothers."*

Job's grief is expressed so eloquently and clearly throughout his story, that one can almost taste the bitterness of his pain. It is also quite clear that he perceives himself to be completely bereft of friendship or support of any kind. Mrs. Job's hurtful words, "Curse God and die" still sting, as he says, "The fact that I am yet breathing offends my wife." But suddenly, here come his brothers and sisters – who most likely had set out from wherever they lived as soon as word had arrived that Job was in trouble and had taken time to travel to where he was. Do not forget, that back then there was no internet, no cell phones, no CNN or Fox News.

For people who lived far away from each other, the only way to communicate was through messages sent by runners or through trade caravans that were headed in the direction of the message's recipient. Job would have had no way to know they were coming, unless they had sent a messenger ahead. He truly believed he was all alone in his suffering. What I love about this is that even while Job was being browbeaten by his wife and his friends, while he lay in a pile of dust and ashes expressing his feelings of pain and grief, he held fast to his faith in a sovereign God. And without his knowledge, God was working for him. His extended family, his support system was on its way to help and care for him even though he had no idea help was on the way.

That is the God we serve! How often have we found ourselves in trouble, in need of assistance, crying out for support and feeling so alone and even abandoned in our time of need, when suddenly help arrives just at that critical time? My dear sister, never forget that God sees ALL. Just as he beheld the suffering and heard the cries of the captives in Egypt and prepared for a deliverer to come and liberate them, he heard the cries of Job, and he saw the despair of Mrs. Job. Even as they wallowed in their grief, each of them in their own way, God had allowed messages to get through to their extended family, who immediately mobilized to be there for them as soon as was possible. We must also believe that God has done, is doing, and will continue to do the same for us.

The Sweetness of Trust: Kezia was the name of the second restored daughter of Job. Kezia or Cassia is a sweet-scented spice; her name in effect means, "Sweet". It recalls the lyrics to the classic hymn, "Tis so sweet to trust in Jesus, just to take Him at His word; just to rest upon His promise, just to know, Thus saith the Lord."

It is indeed sweet to trust in God and to know – just to know – that He is in control. Many

It is Well

times, I have prayed to God and said something along the lines of, "I don't know why You have brought me here, or why I am in this position, nevertheless I will trust in You." And I can say that, without fail, He has never let me down. Help has always come "just in time".

I can recall two distinct occasions during which God has come through for me when I had no other option but to trust Him. The first was many years ago, perhaps a year or eighteen months after my daughter was born. In retrospect, it seems a small thing, but I have come to understand and believe the words of Christ when he said, "if God so clothes the grass of the field, which is alive today and tomorrow is thrown into the furnace, will He not much more clothe you? You of little faith! Do not worry then saying, 'What will we eat? Or What will we drink?" (Matt. 6 v 30-31 NASB) It doesn't matter how insignificant the need is: God is still aware of it and He will supply ALL your needs.

It is Well

We were going through some hard times. I was a full-time university student with a young daughter to care for, and my husband was working in construction, doing "piecework", which means, he got paid by the job. I remember we had run out of milk, which seems a small thing, except we had a baby who needed it. I recall worrying so much about how I would take care of the baby – there was no money for food until my husband's next pay, and I did not feel like there was anyone I could call.

I cried out to the Lord and asked Him to provide for us, and then just left it there. About an hour later, I heard the postman come by and went down to check the mail. There was only one envelope in the mail, and in it was a cheque for $30. It was enough to take care of baby's needs until my husband got paid. It was no grand miracle, but still it was an affirmation of God's interest in my life, and an assurance that He is the God who provides.

It is Well

The second occasion happened almost 30 years after that last story. In 2014 I was privileged to be part of a group of psychology professionals to speak at an international psychology conference in Paris, France. I was so excited to go! My colleagues would be arriving from England, and we were supposed to meet at our shared accommodations in Paris on the same day.

I flew in, then took the metro into the city. Some of the metro lines I was supposed to use to get to my destination were closed for construction, and because I did not know how to use the metro system, I could not find an alternate route. I spent about 45 minutes wandering around the bowels of Paris's metro system before giving up and hailing a cab at street level.

Once the cab arrived at my destination, I realized I now had a new set of problems. My colleagues had not provided me with ALL the information I needed to get into the rented apartment. I had the phone number of the contact; however, my international phone

It is Well

minutes were not working on my phone – I could not get the call to go through. I was in a strange city, stranded outside a building, with no ability to place to call for help. My frenzied texts to my colleagues went unanswered. Unbeknownst to me, they were trapped in the Chunnel due to some malfunction on the train and had no cell service.

I stood outside the apartment building for what felt like forever. I prayed and asked God to intervene and to show me what to do. I was getting to the point where I was ready to just go find a hotel and deal with the rest of it later, and then I was approached by a gentleman on the sidewalk. He asked me in French if I needed assistance. I explained to him my predicament (thank you, Mom and Dad for French Immersion), and told him I could not reach my colleagues, and I couldn't place a call to the landlord to get the keys. In fact, I did not even know which apartment we were supposed to be staying in. He said, "Well I live here. I can at least let you in to the lobby and get you off the street." Once inside, he noted, "The only apartment big enough to house three people is this one on the main floor. It has to be this one."

I thanked him for letting me in. He offered to wait while I attempted to call the landlord again, which I did, to no avail. He correctly surmised that my international plan was a dud. He then offered to let me use his phone. *Now remember, I was in a strange land, and I had been awake for at least 30 hours. I was exhausted. I was scared. I was hungry. And all I wanted to do was have a complete meltdown and perhaps a shower. This man could have been an axe murderer for all I knew, but in that moment, he was all I had in terms of help.* I breathed another prayer asking God for his protection, and replied, "Thank you, that would be very kind."

This stranger, Philippe, carried my 50 lb suitcase up five flights of stairs to his tiny apartment, the size of my living room. He welcomed me into his space, gave me a glass of water, encouraged me to sit down, handed me a phone and walked away. While I made

It is Well

my calls, he worked away in the kitchen prepping food, and when I had finally gotten hold of the landlord who assured me that he would be there within thirty minutes, he again hauled my suitcase back downstairs to the main floor and said goodbye.

Now, if that were the end of the story, we would say, "Yes! God provides. He is an ever-present help in times of trouble." That is true. But there is more. Once I was safe inside my apartment, I had my meltdown and my shower, and set out in search of food. I still had received no word from my colleagues. I stocked up on some essentials, bought a thank you card for Philippe, and wrote a note expressing my gratitude as well as wishes for the blessings of God to be upon his life for his kindness.

Once my colleagues had safely arrived and settled, I headed back up the stairs to leave the card behind. Philippe was so grateful for the card, and exclaimed, "Oh! Julie… come in, come in! We are eating. Please join us!" I wasn't sure what to do, but this person had

It is Well

been so kind, I didn't want to be rude. I came to learn that Philippe and his friend were of the Muslim faith and they were celebrating Ramadan, which meant they fasted from sunup to sundown, and this was their first meal of the day. I further learned that Philippe was a chef at one of the many hotels in Paris, and I was treated to a feast of shrimp bisque, goats cheese brie, veggies and other yummy treats. Again, with my belly full this time, I said my thanks, and went on my way.

It was not until I arrived back in Canada that I was relating the story to one of my Muslim clients, and she said, "Oh, that is one of the things we are encouraged to do during Ramadan. We are to help people in trouble, invite them into our homes, and to ensure they are cared for like family." Even now, as I am writing this, I am overwhelmed to the point of tears with the foresight and the loving providence of God in that situation. He placed Philippe in that building, two years before I ever arrived in Paris, or before my colleagues were directed to that Air BNB apartment. Think of how all the events (my being lost in the metro, my colleagues being stuck in a tunnel under the English Channel, me waiting for and hailing a cab, then standing outside the building before he arrived home and offered to help) came together to ensure that Philippe would be there to help me when I needed it.

Tis so sweet to trust in Jesus!
The name Kezia represents that kind of sweetness that is found in faith in God. It is one thing to BELIEVE in God – to believe that He is. Even the demons believe this, and they tremble at the knowledge! It is something altogether to TRUST God. To put your fate in His hands. To believe that no matter what you see happening around you, that God is still in control. When you can reach that level of trust, what you find there is like peeling back the layers of an onion – it is bitter indeed, and may bring you fountains of tears, but when you get to the center, that is where the sweetness resides, and once you taste that, you know that all the effort was worth it.

It is Well

Strength and Comfort: Kerenhappuch, the name of Job's third restored daughter means Horn of antimony. Now, that sounds like a strange name for a child, particularly a girl child. Maybe we should call her Keren for short. Antimony was used in ancient times as a cosmetic and was named after the Greek words, *anti* and *monos* to mean "a metal not found alone".

As I researched what this could mean, I came across a question asking, "What is the strongest metal in the world?" The answers were interesting, as I discovered, but by themselves they were not revelatory. Then I learned about metal strengths. All combined, this information revealed the amazing insight and power of God to teach us his ways through a study of the natural world.

The strongest metals are steels and alloys – in other words, metals that are combined in order to bolster their strength. Carbon steels are impact-resistant. Maraging steels have incredible yield strength. Stainless steel has high yield and tensile strength, and when combined with nickel, it becomes corrosion resistant. Tool steels are alloyed with cobalt and tungsten and have high impact strength. Finally, inconel, a superalloy of austenite, nickel, and chromium can endure extreme conditions and high temperatures.

Here's where my mind was blown. Job said in Ch 23 v 11, "He knoweth the way that I take: when he hath tried me, I shall come forth as gold." Gold is not the strongest metal; however, once refined, it may be one of the purest. Job understood that his trial was one of fire, and that only God's strength would pull him through.

With respect to metals and alloys, there are four different types of strengths:
    a. Compressive strength describes a metal's ability to withstand compaction or size reduction. It is a measure of how much resistance that metal has when pressed or squeezed.
    b. Tensile strength refers to a metal's ability to resist tension, or a measure of

how much strength would be required to stretch or tear it apart.
c. Yield strength describes how well a material resists deformation, or the strength required to bend that metal.
d. Impact strength describes a metal's ability to resist sudden force or impact without breaking or shattering[i].

When crisis or tragedy comes into our lives it often feels like we are overwhelmed by a flood, pressured to the point of collapse, burdened down with the weight of the world, or that our hearts are being torn apart. But with God, when we are pressed on every side, He is our *compressive* strength. When we feel as though we are being torn to pieces, He is our *tensile* strength. When the cares of life weigh us down, try to bend or break us, the Psalmist says, we "shall be like a tree planted by the rivers of water" (Psalms 1 v 3); God is our *yield* strength. When our worlds come crashing down around us and we are impacted by a sudden force of crisis or chaos, God is our *impact* strength!

It is Well

In trying times, we find this strength in the Word.

2 Corinthians 4 v 7-9: But we have this treasure in earthen vessels, that the excellency of the power may be of God, and not of us. We are troubled on every side, yet not distressed; we are perplexed, but not in despair; persecuted, but not forsaken; cast down but not destroyed.

Romans 8 v 31: What shall we say then to these things? If God be for us, who can be against us?
V 35: Who shall separate us from the love of Christ? Shall tribulation or distress, or persecution, or famine, or nakedness, or peril, or sword? As it is written, 'For thy sake we are killed all the day long; we are accounted as sheep for the slaughter'. Nay in all these things we are more than conquerors through Him that loved us. For I am persuaded that neither death, nor life, nor angels, nor principalities, nor powers, nor things present, nor things to come, nor height, nor depth, nor any other creature,

It is Well

shall be able to separate us from the love of God which is in Christ Jesus our Lord.

Psalm 21 v 1 The king shall joy in thy strength, O Lord; and in thy salvation how greatly shall he rejoice!

Job 41 v 22 In his neck remaineth strength, and sorrow is turned into joy before him.

Nehemiah 8 v 10 Go your way, eat the fat, and drink the sweet, and send portions unto them for whom nothing is prepared: for this day is holy unto our Lord: neither be ye sorry; for the joy of the Lord is your strength.

Proverbs 31 v 25 Strength and honour are her clothing; and she shall rejoice in time to come.

Psalms 28 v 7 The Lord is my strength and my shield.

Phil. 4 v 13 I can do all things through Christ which strengtheneth me.

It is Well

2 Corinthians 12 v 9 My grace is sufficient for thee: for my strength is made perfect in weakness.

Isaiah 40 v 29-31 He giveth power to the faint; and to them that have no might he increaseth strength. Even the youths shall faint and be weary, and the young men shall utterly fall: but they that wait upon the Lord shall renew their strength; they shall mount up with wings as eagles; they shall run, and not be weary; and they shall walk, and not faint.

Psalms 18 v 1 I will love thee, O Lord, my strength.

Eph. 6 v 10 Finally my brethren, be strong in the Lord, and in the power of His might.

Isaiah 41 v 10 Fear thou not; for I am with thee: be not dismayed; for I am thy God: I will strengthen thee; yea, I will help thee; yea, I will uphold thee with the right hand of my righteousness.

It is Well

Be encouraged, my friend! There is nothing on this planet that can crush, smash, pull apart, or break the chosen anointed of God! Let us say with confidence, even as the Apostle Paul declared in 2 Corinthians 12 v 10, "Therefore I take pleasure in infirmities, in reproaches, in necessities, in persecutions, in distresses for Christ's sake: for when I am weak, then am I strong. God is your strength!

Keren's name represented strength and comfort. I believe choosing this name was Job's way of expressing the strength he had through faith in his God; perhaps it was his way of thanking God for remaining with him and strengthening him through his lengthy trial. I believe Keren's name signified God's omnipresence and sovereignty in Job's life. He knew that no matter what, he was never alone. Grab hold of this promise for the situation in which you and your family find yourselves. Remember that God is your strength, and with Him in your life, He is fighting your battles with you and for you! Be comforted in knowing you are never alone.

It is Well

3

WHEN FAITH DIES

1 Kings 17 v 8-16 reads: And the word of the LORD came unto him (Elijah), saying,
"Arise, get thee to Zarephath, which belongeth to Zidon, and dwell there: behold, I have commanded a widow woman there to sustain thee". So, he arose and went to Zarephath. And when he came to the gate of the city, behold, the widow woman was there gathering of sticks: and he called to her, and said, "Fetch me, I pray thee, a little water in a vessel, that I may drink".

And as she was going to fetch it, he called to her, and said, "Bring me, I pray thee, a morsel of bread in thine hand". And she said, "As the LORD thy God liveth, I have not a cake, but an handful of meal in a barrel, and a little oil in a cruse: and, behold, I am gathering two sticks, that I may go in and dress it for me and my son, that we may eat it, and die".

It is Well

And Elijah said unto her, "Fear not; go and do as thou hast said but make me thereof a little cake first, and bring it unto me, and after make for thee and for thy son. For thus saith the LORD God of Israel, 'The barrel of meal shall not waste, neither shall the cruse of oil fail, until the day that the LORD sendeth rain upon the earth'".

And she went and did according to the saying of Elijah: and she, and he, and her house, did eat many days. And the barrel of meal wasted not, neither did the cruse of oil fail, according to the word of the LORD, which he spake by Elijah.

The nameless widow seemed to be a prudent and practical woman. She knew the famine was not going to let up anytime soon. The fields were dry, and the water sources were also drying up. She had little in the way of money and eventually that too ran out. When the prophet had come to her, she only had enough left for one last meal, after which, she planned the unimaginable – to do nothing except to watch her son and herself fade away due to hunger and thirst.

I remember the first time I spoke about this widow, and I flippantly described her faith as "simple". Immediately as I said the word, I was checked in my spirit and I took it back. There is nothing simple about faith when life hangs in the balance. She had to weigh and consider her choices. She could either make that last meal for herself and her son, thereby extending their lives for perhaps a few more days; or she could do as the prophet had asked and make him a meal first. If the prophet's God didn't come through for her, she would essentially be signing her and her son's own death warrants. Yet, despite the immense risk, she chose to do as the prophet had asked. In return, God blessed her household and throughout the duration of the famine and the drought, she and her son were never hungry again.

Despite the wondrous miracle that God continued to perpetuate in the widow's home, something happened to change how she applied her faith. One of the things I notice when I read this passage of scripture is that she responded to the prophet with the words, "As the Lord **THY** God liveth..." (emphasis mine). This causes me to wonder if she did not recognize the Lord God as *her* God. The second thing I wonder is how often she had seen the prophet work miracles in their community while he was a guest in her home. Perhaps it was that she had become **accustomed to the miraculous**. She might have begun to take God's providence for-granted. The third question I have is about her motivation for keeping the prophet in her home. I wonder if she hoped to keep the providence of God present in her home by housing and feeding the prophet. Perhaps she felt that was what *she owed him* since he had ensured she and her son would never run out of food. Or maybe she believed that God's grace evidenced what *she was owed* in her life because of the sacrifice she made for the prophet. Speculation aside, the faith she showed when she baked the cake had transformed into something different by the time the story picked up in verse 17.

It is Well

(1 Kings 17 v 17-24) And it came to pass after these things, that the son of the woman, the mistress of the house, fell sick; and his sickness was so sore, that there was no breath left in him. And she said unto Elijah, "What have I to do with thee, O thou man of God? art thou come unto me to call my sin to remembrance, and to slay my son?" And he said unto her, "Give me thy son". And he took him out of her bosom, and carried him up into a loft, where he abode, and laid him upon his own bed.

And he cried unto the LORD, and said, "O LORD my God, hast thou also brought evil upon the widow with whom I sojourn, by slaying her son?" And he stretched himself upon the child three times, and cried unto the LORD, and said, "O LORD my God, I pray thee, let this child's soul come into him again". And the LORD heard the voice of Elijah; and the soul of the child came into him again, and he revived. And Elijah took the child and brought him down out of the chamber into the house and delivered him unto his mother: and Elijah said, "See, thy son liveth". And the woman said to Elijah, "Now by this I know that thou art a man of God, and that the word of the LORD in thy mouth is truth".

What we know from the telling of the story is that this widowed single mother had been taking care of the prophet Elijah for months. He had worked a great miracle in her house (in response to her great faith), ensuring that there would be food for her and her son for as long as the famine lasted. But then her son became very ill, slipped into a coma and was on the verge of death.

In that moment, her faith crumbled to dust. Her response was one of blaming the prophet and wallowing in self-pity. "What have I done to **you**, prophet? Have you come to remind me of my sins and to kill my son?"

In great distress, Elijah took the boy from her, stretched himself out on the child three times while crying out to God for his life. Suddenly the boy regained consciousness, and Elijah returned him to his mother alive and alert. Then the woman responded in great relief, "NOW I know you are a man of God, and that the word of the Lord in your mouth is TRUTH."

NOW I KNOW…
These three words haunt me every time I read this accounting of God's mercy and grace in the widow's life. "Now I know…" Are we to believe that she did not already know that God was God when the Lord provided food for her household every day? Did she seriously not see the miracles God was performing through the prophet within her community? Did she not truly believe Elijah was a man of God before? Did she really think him to be a liar?

I get it. I do. I understand that she had already lost much. She had lost her husband. She had only one son. Should her son die, the family name would die with him. He was the only one there who would care for her in her latter years. Without him she would be completely destitute, with no hope for her future. Still, how did she get to the place where those words, "Now I know…" made sense for her?

Let's return to the questions posed earlier. Perhaps the widow did *not* know for certain that God was God before she met the prophet. It is not right to assume that everyone in the nation of Israel at the time of the famine believed in God or trusted in Him. We know nothing of the woman's past except that she was a widow and she had a son. God provided her for the prophet, but the Word does not say anything to indicate that she was a God fearer. Surely though, she must have developed some faith in God when she saw that the barrel of meal and the cruise of oil never went empty day after day after day. Maybe – maybe not.

It is possible that she felt comfortable enough just having the prophet in her home, believing that so long as *he* was there, the miracle would perpetuate. She might not have ever come to realize that the miracle was a response to her act of faith and not a function of the prophet's continued presence in her home.

It could be that whatever miracles she witnessed the prophet performing were attributed to *him* and not to the God he served. Maybe there were whispers of doubt in her mind that questioned the prophet's relationship with God. *He could just be a conjurer or a magician. There are other prophets, shamans, holy men who follow other gods… How do I know his God is the real deal? Will the food continue to appear if I let him leave?* Perhaps she wondered why God would supply her and her son with food to last the duration of the famine, only for her son to die from a sickness. Whatever her mindset, one thing is for certain: she needed *proof* that God was able to deliver her and her son.

It is Well

4
BITTER WATERS

The children of Israel had just crossed over the Red Sea and God had wrought a great victory on their behalf. Pharaoh and the armies of Egypt had drowned in the sea, while Moses and the Israelites had miraculously crossed over on dry land. They were so enthralled by the amazing providence of God that they sang songs, played their instruments, danced and gave praise for what Jehovah God had done.

Exodus 15 v 21: And Miriam answered them, "Sing ye to the LORD, for he hath triumphed gloriously; the horse and his rider hath he thrown into the sea." For 21 verses, Exodus 15 shares the praises of Israel for what the Lord their God did at the Red Sea. Then immediately following this record of celebration for God's deliverance, we see that Moses lead the nation into the Wilderness of

Shur, where there was no readily available water, and just like that, the people begin to murmur.

Exodus 15 v 23-24 And when they came to Marah, they could not drink of the waters of Marah, for they were bitter: therefore, the name of it was called Marah. And the people murmured against Moses, saying, "What shall we drink?"

Only a few days journey following yet another great show of strength and power by the almighty God, and the children of Israel were already complaining. Now to be fair, God had done much to demonstrate to the Israelites His ability to overcome their physical enemies, and to preserve them from His judgement. He had shown himself to be Jehovah-Nissi, the God who delivers, but he had not yet fully reassured them that He was also Jehovah-Jireh – the God who provides. In this first account of the Israelites complaining about lack of water, they arrived at a stream, but the waters were sulfuric and bitter. God's solution was simple. Chop down a certain tree and cast it into the water. Moses acted in obedience, and the waters became sweet. Problem solved. Point made. God provides. Simple lesson, right?

Exodus 17 begins like this:
Exodus 17 v 1-7 And all the congregation of the children of Israel journeyed from the Wilderness of Sin, after their journeys, according to the commandment of the LORD, and pitched in Rephidim: and there was no water for the people to drink. Wherefore the people did chide with Moses, and said, "Give us water that we may drink". And Moses said unto them, "Why chide ye with me? wherefore do ye tempt the LORD?" And the people thirsted there for water; and the people murmured against Moses, and said, **"Wherefore is this that thou hast brought us up out of Egypt, to kill us and our children and our cattle with thirst**?"

And Moses cried unto the LORD, saying, "What shall I do unto this people? they be almost ready to stone me." And the LORD said unto Moses, "Go on before the people, and take with thee of the elders of Israel; and thy rod, wherewith thou smotest the river, take in thine hand, and go. Behold, I will stand before thee there upon the rock in Horeb; and thou shalt smite the rock, and there shall come water out of it, that the people may drink". And Moses did so in the sight of the elders of Israel. And he called the name of the place Massah, and Meribah, because of the chiding of the children of Israel, and because they tempted the LORD, saying, Is the LORD among us, or not?

The children of Israel (moms included) were complaining yet again, about their "plight" in the wilderness. Clearly, they did not realize that it was better to be hungry and free than it was to be full but a slave. They did not appreciate, nor did they remember the many times that God had already miraculously provided for their needs. These parents (moms included) focused on what they lacked rather than what had been provided. They turned on Moses as they often did, looking for someone to blame for their thirst. The names Moses assigned to that place were meant to be a challenge to Israel to not lose hope in

It is Well

their God: "Do you trust God, or don't you? Is He with us or not?"

Fast forward several years and sadly, not much had changed. A common adage is one thing that we can learn from history is that we do not learn from history. This appears to be true of the post-Egypt Israelites. Too soon, as was their way, the children of Israel found themselves in another thirsty place. Again, they blamed their leadership and brought on the drama associated with blaming, shaming, and complaining.

Numbers 20 starting at verse 3 says the following: And the people chode with Moses, and spake, saying, "Would God that we had died when our brethren died before the LORD! And why have ye brought up the congregation of the LORD into this wilderness, that we and our cattle should die there? And wherefore have ye made us to come up out of Egypt, to bring us in unto this evil place? it is no place of seed, or of figs, or of vines, or of pomegranates; neither is there any water to drink."

It is Well

And Moses and Aaron went from the presence of the assembly unto the door of the tabernacle of the congregation, and they fell upon their faces: and the glory of the LORD appeared unto them. And the LORD spake unto Moses, saying, "Take the rod, and gather thou the assembly together, thou, and Aaron thy brother, and speak ye unto the rock before their eyes; and it shall give forth his water, and thou shalt bring forth to them water out of the rock: so thou shalt give the congregation and their beasts drink." And Moses took the rod from before the LORD, as he commanded him.

And Moses and Aaron gathered the congregation together before the rock, and he said unto them, "Hear now, ye rebels; must we fetch you water out of this rock?" And Moses lifted up his hand, and with his rod he smote the rock twice: and the water came out abundantly, and the congregation drank, and their beasts also. And the LORD spake unto Moses and Aaron, "Because ye believed me not, to sanctify me in the eyes of the children of Israel, therefore ye shall not bring this congregation into the land which I have given them."

So much can be said of this portion of scripture, but I want to examine it strictly from the point of view of parents concerned for their children and their families. Why did they continue to harp and nag at Moses? What was it that made them feel like it was "okay" to blame the leadership for the situations in which they found themselves? There is a culture within some churches that fosters this type of thinking. When something goes wrong in the marriage, blame the leadership. When a child takes a wayward route away from God, blame the pastor. When faith begins to waver, blame the church.

Let's not forget that the children of Israel wandered the desert for 40 years because of the choices they made. They had bred into themselves a culture of complaining. This negative, never-satisfied attitude took root while they were still in captivity. The Word tells us that for the 400 years that Israel was captive, they moaned and complained and cried out to God until He was moved to send them a deliverer. That is not to say that God ignored them for 400 years, but we must remember that God ALWAYS has a plan. Always.

The challenge for the Israelites was that once they were saved from their captivity, they did not know how to be anything else but complainers. They were so conditioned to complaining, that they could not see the blessings that were right before their eyes!

A 2016 research report that caught the attention of the Globe and Mail[ii] confirms that people who complain a lot re-wire their brains to be more pessimistic and negative. In other words, complaining begets more complaints and makes them more likely to complain about things in the future. Over time, people who complain often find it is easier to be negative than to be positive, regardless of what is truly happening. With time, and no change in behaviour, complaining becomes the default behavior. This is what happened to the children of Israel. They re-wired their brains until complaining was their default response. Sure, they praised God immediately after great victories, but they did not cultivate an attitude of praise and gratitude. Without consistent and conscious attention to their thought lives, they quickly reverted to their old ways of complaining despite the blessings all around them.

Return with me to the story of the widow who had her son restored to her.
I wonder how much she had complained about her lack of food and water and lamented that there was no one to help her in the days before she met the prophet. I wonder if she had also cultivated a complaining and blaming nature like her ancestors had while they were in captivity and in the desert.

It seems clear that her relationship with God was in question. Unlike Job's wife, the widow had a measure of faith, and was willing to act on it at one time; however, her faith was not enough to sustain her when tragedy struck her in a more personal way. The widow lashed out at the person who was closest to her – in this case, the prophet himself. She did not go to him to seek his assistance; rather, she turned on him and blamed him for her misfortune, just as the children of Israel in generations before her had done.

When her son was restored to life, she expressed no gratitude. Rather, she only gave a cursory nod to the fact that Elijah was not a liar, and that he was indeed God's man. The bitter woman lashes out when she is in pain. She blames and seeks to transfer her shame onto those around her. She complains about her circumstances, her lack of resources and supports, and about how alone she is in her condition. She has a glaring lack of empathy and is unable to care for or contribute to the needs of others because she is so steeped in her own misfortune. She cannot connect with others, not in a way that helps her to feel love and belonging. The bitter woman, having lost what made her significant feels lost, like a ship adrift on the ocean. Without enduring faith, she may lose her sense of certainty. If she cannot trust God, then can she trust anything?

5
A Bitter Taste in Her Mouth

There are many theoretical models in the field of psychology and sociology that attempt to explain why humans do what they do. In high school we all learn about Maslow's hierarchy of needs, but Maslow's model is only one of many. One of the models I favour was developed by Anthony Robins, and in it he describes Six Human Needs that are universal in nature but are paradoxical in nature. They are not placed in a hierarchy like Maslow's needs; rather, Robins acknowledges that every human needs all six things, albeit in different measure. The first four needs, he describes as "the needs of the personality".

The first need is the need for Certainty. Certainty is about knowing that you are safe, that your basic needs for food, shelter, and financial sustenance are being met. It is about being in your comfort zone, predictability, uniformity, and consistency. We all need to have a sense of certainty in our lives. Without it, we might feel adrift like a rudderless ship.

The second is the need for Variety. The challenge of having too much certainty is that we can easily become bored. Variety is all about the unpredictable, the spontaneous, the unexpected, the surprise. Variety, as they say, is the spice of life. It keeps life interesting, and it prevents us as human beings from becoming stuck in a rut.

The third is the need for Love and Connection. We need to feel like we belong and that we are connected to something greater than ourselves. No man or woman is an island, right? We seek out ways to fulfill this need by joining clubs, being part of a faith community, playing in league sports, taking classes at the gym, seeking friendships and intimate relationships.

The fourth is the need for Significance. Significance can be explained as finding that thing that makes us *unique*. Often my clients will describe their struggle in discovering their *purpose*. Our significance is what sets us apart from others, that makes us special. One can see how the need for love and connection might conflict with the need for significance. If you are too unique, you might have difficulty forming meaningful connections with others. If you are too enmeshed in collective culture, you might begin to lose sight of who you are as an individual. Just as we must strike a balance between our need for certainty and our need for variety, we must do the same with the needs of love and connection and significance.

These four needs are followed by two "Spirit Needs":
The fifth is the need for Growth and the sixth is the need for Contribution. The way I see it, growth occurs when we have people pouring into our lives. We all need teachers, examples, mentors, benefactors, and leaders; we need

It is Well

Sherpas, experienced navigators to show us the way as we journey through life. Growth happens when we invest in ourselves, when we take the time to reflect on what we have learned and apply those lessons to our lives. Growth occurs when we commit to being better, and we take active steps towards making that commitment a reality. Contribution is all about giving back, paying it forward, and sharing our resources, whether they be financial, emotional, intellectual, spiritual, or material. Contribution is about helping others grow.

Our Spirit needs cannot be met when we are bitter. We cannot grow because bitterness is a weed that chokes out healthy development. If we do not grow, we cannot bear fruit; therefore, we cannot contribute.

The widow's contribution was solely for the purpose of ensuring that her personality needs would be met – the need for certainty (that they would have food), the need for variety (you never knew what the prophet would do), the need for significance (the prophet lived at *her* house, giving her status in the community), and his presence and God's consequent providence ensured that her son would not die of starvation (love and connection).

Had her Spirit needs been a focus of her attention, she would have taken advantage of the prophet's presence in her home in a different way. Think of Mary and Martha, the sisters of Lazarus who, whenever Jesus came to visit their home in Bethany, both catered to his needs (contribution) and sat at his feet to learn from him (growth). **Spirit needs**. Think of the woman at the well in Samaria who, when she perceived Jesus was a prophet, she began asking him questions about God (growth). Think of how she not only drew water for him, but once he spoke into her life, she brought other villagers to him so that they too could learn from him and receive blessing (contribution). **Spirit needs.**

The widow is not recorded as having shared anything more than food and lodging with the prophet. Her focus was not on her spiritual needs; rather, she was fully attending to her personality needs – the needs of NOW, the needs of SELF. She ignored what was important in favour of what was urgent and immediate. It is no wonder then, that when her son fell sick that she would blame the prophet. After all, she had been doing all this for *him*, wasn't she? If the prophet had food and shelter, she could be assured that she and her son would survive the famine.

Had she been focused on her spiritual growth, she might have stepped back for a moment and reasoned with herself: *God must have a plan – even in this. Why would He provide food enough to sustain us through the famine if He intended for my son to die? Surely, He has worked great miracles before, He can do it again.*

6
MAKING BITTER BETTER

If we want to step out of the bitter places in our lives, we must learn to temper the bitter with the other flavours of life. That means we need the sweet and the salty, the sour and the tangy, the spicy and the pungent. We even crave that indescribable enhancement of all flavours called "umami", which is most often made possible by the addition of FAT. Just as man cannot live by bread alone, so can we not subsist only on a diet of bitterness.

In my younger years, when my husband and I were still newlyweds, we struggled with maintaining financial stability. We became parents a little over a year after we were married, and we needed to quickly adjust to the demands of "adulting". Early in those times, when we were faced with one crisis or another, I realized that keeping a positive attitude, and a faith-filled outlook was essential for making it through hard times. I learned to look inward, not in the sense of intense navel gazing; rather, in the way that I would examine my motives and my intentions. I learned to question my choices, and to objectively reflect on how my decisions had created my current outcomes. That doesn't mean that I didn't engage in blaming, shaming, and complaining from time to time. I just knew I couldn't stay there if I wanted to move forward and achieve better outcomes.

I was still in my 20s when I learned about Reality Therapy, developed by Dr. William Glasser, who conceptualized Choice Theory. One of the things I learned about that I still use today, is the art of self-evaluation. Again, this is not about being selfish or egocentric; instead, self-evaluation is a conscious practice of checking in with oneself to ensure that perceptions, expectations, beliefs and actions are fully grounded. I apply the art of self-evaluation daily, but there are some key questions that are crucial to ask of ourselves, when we are in crisis.

1. **What is happening?** Too often, we make *assumptions* about what is going on around us, and we rely on our gut reactions, which may be rooted in past trauma, hurts, poor self-image, communication that was lost in translation, and any other of the myriad of perceptual filters that cause us to guess wrongly. When we step back from our situation and look at it through a lens of "just the facts", without judgment or layering it with our own values or experience, we can identify exactly what the challenge is.

2. **What's good about this?** When your life is spiralling down into the 7th circle of Hell, it may be difficult to find anything at all that you could call "good about this". However, it is crucial that this question be part of the self-evaluation process. Even if you can spot nothing good about your situation in the moment, the beauty of your brain and its complex systems is that, your

brain will immediately set about the task of attempting to answer the question. It will stop focusing on the things you instinctively want to complain about and shift towards seeking out those aspects of your situation that are worthy of gratitude. Often, it will be the answers to this question that keeps you from falling into the depths of despair. Asking and answering this question will help to keep your faith strong, and it will give you courage in those moments when you would otherwise faint from fear.

3. **What can I learn from this?** Michael Scott said, "The day you stop learning is the day you die." I agree. When you stop learning, you stop growing. I have always been of the mind that if everything happens for a reason, I must learn the purpose of my trial. If I learn nothing from my experiences, then the challenges I have faced in my life were for nothing. If I wish to grow, then I must *learn* from what God allows me to go through.

4. **What is God showing me about myself through this trial?** Psalm 139 v 23-24 comes to mind, "Search me, O God, and know my heart: try me, and know my thoughts: and see if there be any wicked way in me and lead me in the way everlasting. Whenever I find myself in a time of crisis, I find myself praying this prayer. "God, what do you want of me? What do you want me to learn? How do you want me to grow? Who in my future might benefit from the lessons you are teaching me now? What is your plan for my life? What in my life must change for me to survive this trial and come forth like gold?"

Sometimes my clients will ask me if I believe that the bad things happening in their lives are because God is punishing them for something they did in their past. Personally, I don't believe that is how God works. I believe that the rain falls on the just and the unjust, and I too am sometimes flabbergasted by the weight of burden some are required to bear. Even so, I do not believe that God sits up on his throne in heaven wielding a baseball bat, waiting for us to mess up so that he can whack us with it. If you believe that God has a purpose for your life, then ask this question and trust Him to provide the answers.

5. **What is God showing me about Himself through this trial?** Let me tell you something, this is one of the greatest questions we can ask if we want to avoid becoming bitter in our crisis. These questions overlap and compliment each other. What is good about this? God is good. What can I learn from this? I can learn things about myself. I can learn more about my Heavenly Father.

God might wish for you to have a deeper understanding of his provision, of his ability and power to heal; to learn more about His saving grace or His delivering hand. He may want you to finally come to the realization that no matter what, He loves you with an everlasting love. He may want you to accept His forgiveness and truly claim it for your life. Trust that through the fire, He is standing with you, and He will reveal something of Himself that will empower you in the days to come.

Search Me O God
Search your heart. Are there things about your trial that are leaving a bitter taste in your mouth? Reach out to your Father while engaging in some sincere self-evaluation. Doing so is vital to fortify yourself against falling into the trap of perpetual complaining.

Performing the act of self-evaluation is essential to your Spirit needs. To grow and contribute, you must be aware of the areas in your life that are lacking. Likewise, you must ensure that your cup is full enough that you can contribute to the needs of others. Can you pray for others when you are in the throes of distress? Do you have empathy for those around you who are also struggling? Can you be like Job who said, "The Lord gives, and He takes away. Blessed be His name"?

It is Well

Are you willing to leave off complaining, shaming, and blaming? Are you willing to put your faith and hope in God and stop putting your faith in fallible man? Are you willing to focus on your Spirit needs even when your Personality needs are not being met? Saying YES to all these questions will set you firmly on the road from Bitter to Better.

It is Well

PART TWO

Better

It is Well

It is Well

7

99 Bottles of Oil on the Wall

2 Kings 4 v 1-7 relates the following story. Another widow approached another prophet. She cried out to Elisha, "My husband is dead, and now the creditor has come to take my sons away to be his slaves!"

"What do you have in the house?" He asked her urgently.

Despondently, she replied, "I have nothing. Except a jar of oil."

"Quickly now," he said to her, "Go and borrow as many pots as you can find. Every single one – send your sons too!"

It is Well

While they were busy gathering vessels, he set up an assembly line. Once they had all they could find, he closed the door tight, and commanded the widow to pour the small jar of oil into the first vessel. Miraculously, the oil continued to pour until every last vessel was FULL!

"Go now and sell the oil to pay your debt, and you and your boys can live on the rest." The crisis was averted, thanks to a quick-thinking prophet, an obedient family, and a faithful, miracle working God.

What a difference between this widow and the one whose son was saved by the prophet, Elijah! This widow's desperation was just as palatable, the urgency just as intense. Her two sons' lives were at stake, her family was going to be broken up because of debt. She would likely have been left destitute and without means had both of her sons been taken from her to be sold into indentured servitude. What I love about this widow is her obedience and that of her sons. They did not stand idly by, while watching their mother try to save the day; rather, they jumped in, and were also obedient to the prophet, following their mother's example.

The second difference between this woman and the widow in Elijah's life is her relationship with God. 2 Kings 4 v 1 says that she was a wife of the son of a prophet. Her husband was known to Elisha. She had married into a family of prophets and she knew and embraced the God of her forbears. She knew that Elisha was the man to turn to, not because he could do anything for her *as a man*, but she knew that he would be able to hear from God and receive and answer for her situation.

The miracle of the never emptying cruise of oil meant that the family was not only provided for in the immediate, but their social status would have also been elevated. Once a lowly widow with two sons scraping to get by while burdened under debts accrued by her late husband, she now found herself in a position to pay off her debts and take on the role of merchant, selling the oil, a precious commodity, and guaranteeing a better quality or a higher standard of living for her entire family. Whereas Elijah's widow was able to maintain her meager quality of life throughout the duration of the famine, this widow and her sons' quality of life was forever changed and improved.

This woman did not resort to blaming, complaining, or shaming. She did not attack the prophet, nor did she blame God for her misfortune. She assertively stated her need, AND she responded in faith.

The similarity I do notice between the two widows is this: in both cases, there is no record of either woman expressing gratitude for the life-saving miracles they received. We might assume that in both instances these mothers would have been extremely grateful; however, the words, "Now I know..." still resonate in my ears. This second widow expressed sudden revelation of God and His power – she already knew who He was and what He was capable of. What is notable though, is that there is no indication of her gratitude to God or to the prophet. She just took her miracle and moved on.

The nine lepers in Luke 17 v 19 were like this. And as [Jesus] entered into a certain village, there met him ten men that were lepers, which stood afar off: and they lifted up their voices, and said, "Jesus, Master, have mercy on us".

And when he saw them, he said unto them, "Go shew yourselves unto the priests". And it came to pass, that, as they went, they were cleansed. And one of them, when he saw that he was healed, turned back, and with a loud voice glorified God, and fell down on his face at his feet, giving him thanks: and he was a Samaritan.

And Jesus answering said, "Were there not ten cleansed? but where are the nine? There are not found that returned to give glory to God, save this stranger." And he said unto him, "Arise, go thy way: thy faith hath made thee whole."

It is Well

All ten lepers cried out for help. They were all obedient to the Lord's command, but nine of them didn't recognize the miracle they had received. They did not stop to give thanks. What is interesting and beautiful about this tale is that Jesus gave a double portion of healing to the one thankful leper when he said, "Arise, and go thy way. Thy faith hath made thee whole" (Luke 17:19). It is like this: the nine lepers were cleansed, but they would still bear the scars of their disease. Sure, they would be able to return home to their families after performing all the necessary rituals as per the law, but they would never be the same again. The physical reminders of their sickness would always be visible to them and to those around them. But for leper number ten, his faith and his *gratitude* made him completely WHOLE. No more scars, no visible reminders of his disease. All that he had lost to leprosy would be restored. It's amazing what praising can do!

Why is it so hard to say, "Thank YOU?"
After thousands of years, human nature has not changed. Many times, people walk

through church doors praying for a miracle. They demonstrate their faith, but once the miracle arrives, they move on. They often don't notify the church that prayed that their miracle was received. I wonder, is it that we have become such an entitled people that we have lost the ability to say "Thanks"? Or have we always been that way? So far, the examples we have explored from the Word of God would suggest that human beings have always been a little slow to show gratitude.

There is also the question of expectations, which may account for this phenomenon of un-thankfulness. Our expectations often influence our emotions and our behaviours. As a parent, you have expectations for your children: they will get up on time, eat their breakfast, go to school. They will study hard, get decent grades, come home after school and do their homework. They may be expected to do chores or help around the house. Typically, the only time they hear about these expectations is when those expectations are *unmet*. I mean, how many of you parents *thank* your children for going to school every day? Yet, we do not hesitate to point out to our children when they have forgotten to complete a chore, or they have received a low grade because they didn't hand in their homework.

We do the same thing in our walk with God. We expect God to provide. We expect Him to be faithful. We expect Him to comfort us and shelter us in times of storm. Likewise, we have expectations of our church leadership. We expect them to be there when we call. We expect them to support us and pray for us when we are in need. Could it be that when we need God to come through for us, or we need the church or the preacher to do something for us, we do not show thankfulness because we *expect* them to do it anyway? After all, why should we say, "Thank You" to someone for doing something they are "supposed to do"?

8
Cultivate an Attitude of Gratitude

If we want to go from Better to Blessed, then perhaps we should start with cultivating an attitude of gratitude. King David understood this, perhaps more than anyone. He had been blessed with much and had lost much; therefore, he often repeated this command in his songs: "*Give thanks* unto the Lord for He is good…"

From bitter grief to abundant blessing
I think of Naomi (Ruth 1), who lost her husband and both her sons. Times were tough. There was a famine in the land. Naomi emigrated from her homeland with her

It is Well

husband Elimelech and her two sons. Her husband died leaving her with her boys, who married daughters of Moab. Then sadly, her sons both died. She was left with daughters not of her blood. When she decided to go back to the land of her birth, she advised her daughters-in-law to return to their homes as she felt she had nothing left to give them. One of the women did as she suggested, but the other refused and promised to stay with her no matter what. And so, they returned to Bethlehem, sorrowing and poor, without a means to provide for themselves.

Naomi claimed her name should be called "Mara" because God had dealt bitterly with her. Was she entitled to feeling bereft? She certainly had a right to grieve.

Despite her pain, look at Ruth chapter 1 v 8 - 13: And Naomi said unto her two daughters in law, "Go, return each to her mother's house: the LORD deal kindly with you, as ye have dealt with the dead, and with me. The LORD grant you that ye may find rest, each of you in the house of her husband". Then she kissed them; and they lifted up their voice and wept.

And they said unto her, "Surely we will return with thee unto thy people".

And Naomi said, "Turn again, my daughters: why will ye go with me? are there yet any more sons in my womb, that they may be your husbands? Turn again, my daughters, go your way; for I am too old to have an husband. If I should say, I have hope, if I should have an husband also to night, and should also bear sons; Would ye tarry for them till they were grown? Would ye stay for them from having husbands? Nay, my daughters; for it grieveth me much for your sakes that the hand of the LORD is gone out against me".

The love and gentleness that is evident in Naomi's words, speaks to her character and the fact that she continued to trust God as her provider. There is an invaluable lesson in Naomi's example. Grieving is not wrong. Questioning God is not wrong. Allowing that grief to overtake you and drench you in bitterness will hurt you and the ones you love and may ultimately destroy your relationship with God.

Call Me Mara:
I don't really believe that Naomi was *bitter* in the way that we interpret the word today. What she said was, "The Lord has dealt with me bitterly." She did not ever say, "I am bitter against the Lord." If you had outlived all your loved ones, you too might feel as though the Lord has dealt bitterly with you. There are deep feelings of grief associated with that kind of loss – grief that cannot be put into words. There are questions: Why? Why were they taken? Why am I still here? So much survivor guilt.

But here's the thing. I believe Naomi found a way to continue to hold fast to her faith in God. The words are not spoken, but the more I review her story, I can almost hear her prayers sounding very much like Job's. "The Lord gives, and He takes away. I don't know why He has taken so much away from me, yet I will trust Him. I know my Redeemer lives;

so, I will go back to the land of my ancestors, and trust in God to provide."

These were not the prayers or thoughts of a *bitter* woman: they were words of one with whom God had dealt bitterly. She understood all too well that life is not always fair, but there would be a season for suffering, and she prayed for a season of restoration.

Imagine the feeling one gets when one is chosen "at random" for a search by airport security. We know it happens, and we see the necessity of it, but when it happens to us, we don't enjoy it so much. We might complain quite effusively about the inconvenience. Then, when the security searches reveal someone who has nefarious intentions, we all heave a sigh of relief, grateful for the inconvenience and the discomfort of the precaution.

Naomi might have been "bitter" at first, and she even tried to have her name changed to Mara, but it didn't stick. How do we know this? The story teller would have changed her name and continued to use the new moniker. That too, speaks to her character – that it did not reflect the bitterness of which she spoke. People still saw her as Naomi. The way she nurtured Ruth and advised her, showed that she was still a mom at heart and that she had much to contribute. Ruth helped Naomi heal, but Naomi also helped Ruth to secure a future.

Ruth Ch 4 v 13-17 reads: So, Boaz took Ruth, and she was his wife: and when he went in unto her, the LORD gave her conception, and she bare a son. And the women said unto Naomi, "Blessed be the LORD, which hath not left thee this day without a kinsman, that his name may be famous in Israel. And he shall be unto thee a restorer of thy life, and a nourisher of thine old age: for thy daughter in law, which loveth thee, which is better to thee than seven sons, hath born him".

And Naomi took the child, and laid it in her bosom, and became nurse unto it. And the women her neighbours gave it a name, saying, "There is a son born to Naomi; and they called his name Obed: he is the father of Jesse, the father of David."

Gratitude makes you better
My mother always told me, "Before you open a gift, read the card, and say thank you to the person who gave you the gift." Likewise, I was forbidden from taking too much pleasure from a gift if I had not first written and sent a Thank You card. Even now, I take as much pleasure in writing Thank You cards as I get in receiving a gift. I enjoy shopping for the cards and writing personalized messages in them. It isn't so much about the shopping for the cards as it is about maintaining an attitude of gratitude.

Consider the children of Israel, having been delivered from slavery, free to move about as they wished, no longer suffering under the lash, complaining about the heat, the dust, the lack of water, the same food every day for years, whining about Moses's leadership and all manner of other things. I wonder how many times those poor parents had to hear, "Are we there yet?" from their kids on that 40-

year pilgrimage. How many mothers buried their children in the desert? How many of them became bitter because of it? How many mothers allowed that spirit of complaining to infect their brains until they could find no joy in their freedom?

The extravagant gift
Many years ago, I heard a sermon preached entitled, "The Extravagant Gift". It was one of those messages that wormed its way into my heart and has remained a part of my psyche ever since. The subject of the message was Mary Magdalene, who broke open a precious jar of scented oil, using it to anoint the feet of Jesus after washing His feet with her tears and drying them with her hair.

Perhaps it is the mental image that this beautiful tale of love, devotion, and gratitude evokes that has caused this message to stay with me all these years. Every time I read this passage of scripture, I am reminded of the life from which Jesus rescued Mary. I think of how her life would have had little value in the eyes of her community until Jesus found her and restored her.

I am reminded of the lyrics penned by Cece Winans in her song, *Alabaster Box,* and I cannot help but think back to when I too, felt I had little value in the eyes of my peers, my church, and my community. In my youth I had made mistakes, I had fallen away from my relationship with God, and I did not feel worthy of His love or salvation. However, even in my sin, Jesus loved me. Before I was a glimmer in my mother's eye, He saw all I would become, and He went to the cross *for me.* Then I too, am compelled to pour out my praise like oil, giving thanks to God for His amazing grace and enduring mercy.

Your gratitude to Christ for his mercy and grace – especially when you find yourself in crisis - is an *extravagant gift*. It has already been established how against human nature, it is to show appreciation and give thanks. How much more difficult is it to maintain an attitude of gratitude when things are dire, and hope is yet to be found? But when we reach down inside of ourselves, and make that "sacrifice of praise", giving thanks to God for who He is and for what He has already done, it increases our faith for what He is yet to do.

The command, "give thanks" is uttered 34 times in the Bible. There are even more references to showing gratitude if we look at every verse that encouraged us to "praise the Lord", or to do other things while giving thanks (such as singing psalms and hymns or remaining in prayer and supplication). Giving thanks is a quintessential aspect of who we are as Christ's followers. The sacrifice of such an extravagant gift as you walk through your trial is one that will not go unnoticed by the Almighty.

You don't have to take my word for it – just look at what the Word of God says about gratitude.

2 Samuel 22 v 50 Therefore I will give thanks unto thee, O LORD, among the heathen, and I will sing praises unto thy name.

It is Well

1 Chronicles 16 v 8 Give thanks unto the LORD, call upon his name, make known his deeds among the people.

1 Chronicles 16 v 34 O give thanks unto the LORD; for he is good; for his mercy endureth for ever.

1 Chronicles 16 v 35 And say ye, "Save us, O God of our salvation, and gather us together, and deliver us from the heathen, that we may give thanks to thy holy name, and glory in thy praise."

Psalms 18 v 49 Therefore will I give thanks unto thee, O LORD, among the heathen, and sing praises unto thy name.

Psalms 30 v 4 Sing unto the LORD, O ye saints of his, and give thanks at the remembrance of his holiness.

Psalms 30 v 12 To the end that my glory may sing praise to thee, and not be silent. O LORD my God, I will give thanks unto thee for ever.

It is Well

Psalms 97 v 12 Rejoice in the LORD, ye righteous; and give thanks at the remembrance of his holiness.

Psalms 105 v 1 O give thanks unto the LORD; call upon his name: make known his deeds among the people.

Psalms 106 v 1 Praise ye the LORD. O give thanks unto the LORD; for he is good: for his mercy endureth for ever. (This command is repeated *nine* times throughout the Word of God!)

Psalms 119 v 62 At midnight I will rise to give thanks unto thee because of thy righteous judgments.

Psalms 140 v 13 Surely the righteous shall give thanks unto thy name: the upright shall dwell in thy presence.

Ephesians 1: v 6 Cease not to give thanks for you, making mention of you in my prayers;

It is Well

Colossians 1 v 3 We give thanks to God and the Father of our Lord Jesus Christ, praying always for you,

1 Thessalonians 1 v 2 We give thanks to God always for you all, making mention of you in our prayers;

1 Thessalonians 5 v 18 In everything give thanks: for this is the will of God in Christ Jesus concerning you.

Give thanks unto the LORD; for he is good; for his mercy endureth for ever!

It is Well

9
FROM BETTER TO BLESSED

Thus far, our study of motherhood in times of crisis has demonstrated the pitfalls of becoming bitter, the benefits of striving to accept the bitter with the sweet, and the need to focus on becoming better through our trials. Bitterness chokes out growth and limits the ability to contribute. Bitterness in no way brings us closer to the fulfillment of our Spirit Needs.

By engaging in conscious self-evaluation and developing an attitude of gratitude, we can move from bitter to better. Through the process of self-reflection, you will notice the salty and sour aspects of your current crisis. Prayerful consideration of what God wants you to learn, be, do, or have as a result of your trial, mixed with an attitude of gratitude, will result in a bursting of new flavours: the sweet, spicy, and savoury, enhanced by the fatness of God's never-ending provision. Remember these words of the psalmist as you forge ahead, "I have never seen the righteous forsaken, nor His seed begging bread" (Psalms 37 v 25).

Even with an attitude of gratitude and a practice of self-evaluation and prayer for God's direction and the accomplishment of His will in my life, sometimes as a mom, it is easy to get bogged down in some universal "Mom Blunders". I think of Sarai, who came up with her own solution for God's promise of a son; or Rebecca, who manipulated her husband and her firstborn so that her favorite son would find favour. Modern day moms are not that different from the moms of old; however, our culture has instilled in us some "super blunders" that act as stumbling blocks between us and our blessing.

It is Well

Mom-Guilt and Self-Blame

The struggle is real! Mom Guilt is a living breathing monster that lurks in the back of every woman's closet, waiting until she has conceived, fostered, or adopted a child to make itself known. Suddenly, we begin to believe that every aspect of our child's existence is dependent on our decisions. That, my friends, is a heavy burden to bear.

It's my fault. If only I had done this or that... what did I do for my child to end up like this? Am I being repaid for my sins?

We moms have a bad habit of taking responsibility for the actions of our children as though it is our fault that they did what they did. I wonder if this tendency started all the way back at the origins of mankind with Eve. Eve made a bad decision, and because of what she and Adam did, sin came into the world. It was that sin that caused Cain to commit murder. It was sin that resulted in both her sons being lost to her forever. But was it Eve's *fault* that Abel was murdered by his brother? Sin was to blame. Cain's bad attitude and poor choices were to blame. Notwithstanding, I don't doubt that Eve spent a great deal of time asking herself the same questions and beating herself up about the role she played in sin entering the world. It is no surprise then, that it took over 100 years for her to conceive and bear another child.

I wonder if Job's wife ever felt guilty for the way she had treated her husband when he was at rock bottom. Did she ever arrive at some level of self-awareness that caused her to feel sorry for what she had said and done in a fit of anger? Did that guilt haunt her long after their riches and their family had been restored?

The thing is, we must accept that although as parents we sometimes make poor decisions, choices that will impact us and our families for years to come, the decisions of our children are theirs and theirs alone. While we may have some influence over the behaviour of others, we do not have the power to "make" anyone do anything that they did not want to do in the first place. Blaming yourself for the choices of your child will not help him, nor will it help you. As painful as this sounds, what is done is done. Do not spend your energy laying blame at your own feet, when that energy could be better spent on your knees.

Mom Shame
Mom Shame is a close kinswoman of Mom guilt. This blunder occurs when moms find themselves embarrassed by the crisis. A daughter gets pregnant. A son gets in trouble with the law. Worrying over "what people will say" can become all consuming, forcing moms to take drastic steps to hiding their shame. In my practice, I see this often, and have been guilty of falling prey to Mom shame on occasion. Seeing the psychological and physiological effects of Mom Shame has alerted me to the dangers of this Mom Blunder. Feeling shame for something that you did not do doesn't make sense; however, because of pervasive and persistent Mom

Guilt, moms will often become convinced that the child's crisis is their fault. If they will believe that lie, then Mom Shame is sure to step in and consume moms' emotions.

Survivor Guilt
Survivor Guilt is another close cousin to Mom Guilt, and one that we moms often encounter. How many times as a mother have you wished or prayed for God to take the pain from your children and give it to you instead? How many moms have suffered intense grief coupled with survivor guilt after a child passes away? *Why God, could you not have taken me and allowed my child to live?*

Again, I cannot help but think of Eve and the crippling pain she must have felt at the loss of her two sons. What a heavy burden to bear! I wish I had some easy answers for survivor guilt, but the truth is that we often will never know the answer of why things happen to our children – why God allowed their crises to occur. What I do know for certain is that God knows the beginning from the ending. He is the author and finisher of our faith, and He is

It is Well

the Alpha and Omega. Know that no matter what He has in store for your children and mine, there's not much we can do (if anything) to change His mind. He is God after all, and we are not. So, what we must do is simply trust Him. And when it seems like survivor guilt would bury us under a burden of pain and suffering, we can do as the Word instructs us in 1 Peter 5 v 7, "casting all [our] care upon Him; for He careth for [us]."

Blame the Child
When a mother is focused solely on her personality needs, sometimes a crisis results in her worrying more about herself than about the needs of her child. Imagine a mom who asks, "How could my child do this to me? He has no idea how his behavior is killing me." These are the words of a selfish, Mrs. Job-like mom. Words that do not demonstrate concern for the child, rather they are words that reflect the mother's belief that everything is about her, as though somehow her child is punishing her by going through a crisis. Trust me when I tell you that your child is not trying to give you a hard time; your child is *having* a

hard time. Pray that God will help you to step outside of yourself, to be filled with compassion for your child, even though you may just want to shut the whole world and focus only on your needs.

Rescuing/Enabling
Trying to prevent your child from experiencing the consequences of his or her own actions is another common Mom Blunder, again fueled by Mom Guilt.

Examples of rescuing or enabling are, giving an addict money when he asks for it. Protecting your child from consequences. Bailing them out of situations they knowingly got themselves into rather than helping them problem solve. Allowing them to come home when they should be in rehab.

Enabling is not the same as doing what you think is right to affect the best outcome for you and your child. I'm talking about running around rescuing the kids so that they never have to experience the pain of learning that their behavior has very real consequences.

It is Well

One of the things I teach in just about every seminar or workshop is this equation: E+R=O. Event plus Response equals Outcome. It is your *decisions,* not your *conditions* that determine your outcomes. When we run around trying to protect our kids from the natural consequences of their behavior, they fail to learn this all-important lesson: to every action, there is an equal and opposite reaction. They cannot expect to steal things and not be punished when they are caught. They cannot cheat on an exam without real consequences. They cannot take reckless risks with their bodies and not expect to have immediate or long-term damage to their health.

Even as I write this, I realize I must be totally transparent and admit that I too, have made the Mom Blunder of rescuing. I was taught by my mother to be a tigress when it comes to my children. There have been times when I have dropped the gloves and "shirted" a few people (figuratively of course) in defense of my children. I stand by *most* of those decisions to fight for my babies, particularly when they were younger and could not fight for themselves.

Now they are adults, and I must constantly remind myself to step aside, wait for them to own up to their mistakes and ask for help rather than jumping in to save the day. I need to remind them that sooner or later they will have to master the art of "adulting". I offer to assist by sharing advice or making suggestions for what to do, rather than just "doing for" them. My friends, I hope some of you are nodding your heads along with me when I tell you *this is hard!* I wish I were independently wealthy so I could throw money at their every need so they would want for nothing. But if I did that, they would never learn to be RESPONSE-ABLE. I need them to develop the skills of response-ability so they can make educated decisions about all the aspects of their lives. Should I die tomorrow, I need to know that my babies will survive on their own.

Even in times of crisis, we must find ways to step back and objectively evaluate what is happening and check ourselves that we are not jumping in to save the day at the expense of our children missing out on important life lessons.

In addition to the Mom Blunders that can be stumbling blocks to receiving our blessing, it is important to address some of the common emotional responses that occur when a tragedy or a crisis is thrust upon us.

Confusion
Confusion is not so much a Mom Blunder as it is a precursor to Mom Guilt and the various types of Blame. When we find ourselves asking, "How did this happen?" it can lead to further questions like, "Is this my fault?" "Is there something I could have done to prevent this?" "Why is this happening to my child?" "I thought God promised He would take care of my children – so what does this mean that my child is in trouble?"

Anger
Certainly, the questions asked while in the throes of confusion can often lead to feelings

of anger. I remember years ago, meeting a woman whose husband had passed away. She was vibrating from head to toe as she expressed how angry she was with him for leaving her alone. I've seen moms devastated by the loss of a child, becoming so angry at the world, at people, at God, at the church, at themselves, that they sink into a pit of bitterness from which they cannot be rescued.

Do not be surprised if throughout the various stages of your crisis, anger makes an appearance. I remember telling a friend that I often struggled between wanting to take my son in my arms and comfort him or punching him in the face. She laughed out loud and said she had felt the same way when she was going through her crisis with her daughter! Anger is a natural and expected response, but we cannot stay there. We must find ways to resolve this volatile emotion, so we don't become consumed by it.

It is Well

Fear

At times during a family crisis, fear can be overwhelming and paralyzing. Fear for your child's safety or survival. Fear of the future. Fear of the unknown. Fear that you might lose your mind. Fear that your child will lose their soul. Fear for your marriage. Fear for your job. Fear that people won't understand. Fear for your health or the health of your partner. Fear that you will never recover even if your child does.

The Word of God tells us often: "FEAR NOT!" In fact, that command is repeated 365 times in the Bible, one for every day of the year.

The Bible references women who faced crippling fear and terrifying circumstances, yet they found the strength and courage to overcome.
- Abigail, whose wisdom saved her family and won her the hand of the king
- Jael the wife of Heber the Kenite, who killed their country's enemy, Sisera with a tent peg and a hammer

- Rahab who saved her entire family from destruction when the walls of Jericho fell

Ladies, give thanks that there are no angry kings with their armies storming down your doors, or enemy forces coming into your home to take advantage of you and your family, or an entire nation getting ready to destroy your neighbourhood or your city. If these women could find strength in the face of their fear, we can dig deep to stand strong despite the intensity of our battles.

Blame Church Leadership or Membership
As I write this section, I feel as though I am navigating a field of IEDs and landmines. Still, I believe it is important to address this issue. Not all church cultures are created equal. Some church leaders are "old school", some are "new school". Some are radically progressive while others are steeped in tradition. Some leaders are well-read, educated, interested in serving the church body in a wholistic way, whereas others are only interested in serving what they perceive

as the "spiritual needs" of their church membership. Some leaders (and this applies to the secular world as well) believe themselves to be great motivators and compassionate counsellors, when in fact they are not at all.

Not all church leaders are going to shine in moments of crisis. Not all church leaders are equipped with the skills that are required to walk alongside people when they are facing the darkest times of their lives. We must remember that while they are spiritual leaders, they are still 100% human beings, which means they are fallible and imperfect.

Blaming the leadership or the church body is a sure-fire way to become bitter. Just as it is not your fault that your children made choices that led them into crisis, neither is it the leadership's fault for what has happened. Church leaders *do* have a responsibility to be good shepherds to their flocks, and I am in no way saying that we should absolve church leadership of that responsibility. I certainly think that it is wise to know and understand the type of church leader you have and reach out to him or her only for the type of support that you know s/he can provide.

Part of the reason why we find ourselves disappointed in and disillusioned by our church family in times of crisis, is that we expect them to intuitively know, anticipate, and meet our needs and those of our struggling family. The thing about expectations is that they are often based on our personal biases of how things *should* be done, rather than the reality of how things *are* done. Right or wrong, expecting people to be or do anything different than what they have always been or done, is a blunder of enormous proportions.

For Church Leadership
For church members and leaders who wonder how they can be of service and assistance to moms in crisis, please be sure to think before you speak. If you're not sure if the word you have for someone is from the Lord, seek His face before you deliver it. Please recognize that not everyone is qualified or empowered

by the Holy Spirit to speak into the life of one who is in crisis.

Know your boundaries and your competencies. If you have no skill as a counsellor, then say so, and refer to someone who has that competency. Coordinate with the resources in your community so you know where to send people with specific needs. We can no longer continue to operate in a bubble as though the pastor or even the leadership team can be all things to all people. Know when you have reached the end of your competency and let the person in crisis know that you are as much out of your depth as they are. Trying to fumble your way through someone else's crisis, trying to be all that you are not, helps no one. I know it is not really *en vogue* for ministers of the gospel to openly admit what they cannot do; however, your honesty and transparency will go further towards establishing your credibility than "faking it till you maybe make it".

The final bit of encouragement I would offer to church leadership is this: Feed your flock,

It is Well

don't beat them. It is easy to fall into some of these blunders from a leadership perspective – to say, "It is this person's own fault for making poor choices, or falling away from God, or for doing this or that." You might even be right. But blaming someone for their misfortune is not only in poor taste, it is also not at all what Jesus would do. If we are His body, we must act as He would have acted. In every case, Jesus reached out to those in crisis with compassion, empathy, and love. He never judged them. In fact, his judgement was reserved primarily for the "religious leaders" of His day. He had no use for self-righteous, judgemental, self-involved, overly pious people. When those of our flock are injured, come up lame, are struggling to stand on their own two feet, or are so crippled by their own circumstances that they must be carried, our job as the body of Christ – your job as the shepherd of your flock – is to carry them, to nurture them, and to do your best to help them become healthy again. If you cannot do that on your own, seek out those who can assist. Blaming the sheep for getting caught in a thicket does not help its rescue.

10

LORD, GIVE ME PATIENCE!

Everybody says, God may not come when you want him but He's always right on time. Well that is fine and good until you are the one who wants Him, and He is slow to show. Then, let me tell you, when you're waiting, nothing feels like the answer is coming on time. Waiting is torture.

The place that my friend, Rev. Jeremy Hanscom calls, "The land of Between" is a difficult place in which to find ourselves. Whether it is weight loss, home renovations, training a new puppy, or completing an educational program, we all want the before and after picture. We want the change to be as instant as looking from the picture on the left to the new improved one on the right.

God doesn't work that way. Sure, there are lots of stories in the Bible where the intervention of God is prefaced by the word, "immediately" or "suddenly". Likewise, there are many more tales of God's slow and steady work. 400 years of slavery. 40 years in Pharoah's house. Another 40 years in the wilderness living as a shepherd. Another 40 years wandering in the wilderness leading the children of Israel to freedom. 40 years of blindness. 7 years of famine. 12 years of uncontrolled bleeding. Four days to respond to a desperate cry for help. Three days in the grave.

"The journey is as important as the destination".
The children of Israel proved this, as did both prophets Elijah and Elisha. How many years did David wait to be crowned king after he was anointed? How many years did Hannah pray for a child before she was blessed with Samuel? How many nights did Nicodemus

fret about the chance he would take in meeting privately with Jesus before he got up the nerve to seek him out? How long did Zaccheus wait in the tree before Jesus found him?

One of the secrets of finding a way to move from better to blessed is to recognize that there is value in the waiting. In the 21st century we don't have to wait for much. We make fun of the rotary phone, dial-up internet, and answering machines. Back in the day, when a bus was late, we had no choice but to wait. There were no cell phones for calling Uber. There was a time before PizzaPizza® came out with their "30 minutes or it's free" policy that we could wait upwards of an hour for our pizza delivery. Now we wait for nothing, or so it would seem. Standing in line at the bank is a thing of the past – we can bank online and do it instantly. Fast food restaurants with drive-thru windows have minimum standards for how quickly drivers can get through ordering and receiving their food.

Sadly, we expect God to be the same. We want Him to adapt to the times. Speed things up. We don't want an "on-time" God anymore – we want a "right-now" God. If we can get everything else that we want in a flash, why shouldn't we have God's blessings in the same way?

There is value in the waiting
When your heart is breaking, and your world seems to be falling apart, waiting doesn't feel like such a great option. In the movies when suspense is palatable, you may only have to wait a few seconds before the rescue comes and even then, it is hard to watch without grabbing the edge of your seat or clenching your fists. When it is your own life or worse, the life of your child, that hangs in the balance, the waiting can be excruciating.

Even so, consider if Moses had not spent 40 years in the desert learning how to trust Jehovah God, he would not have matured enough as a leader to be able to handle what God knew was in his future. What if the woman with the issue of blood had not already spent all she had on doctors who couldn't help? Would she have been desperate enough to press her way through the crowd to Jesus? What if Hannah had gotten a child the first time she prayed? Would she have lent him to the Lord, or would she have responded much like the second widow, and just carried on her merry way? What if Jesus had just spoken a word and healed Lazarus from a distance? Would the people of Bethany have come to know that He had the power to raise the dead? Would Mary have received the revelation of Jesus as the resurrection and the life?

There is blessing in waiting! The Word reminds us of this often:

Psalms 37 v 9 For evildoers shall be cut off: but those that wait upon the LORD, they shall inherit the earth.

Isaiah 30 v 18 And therefore will the LORD wait, that he may be gracious unto you, and therefore will he be exalted, that he may have mercy upon you: for the LORD is a God of

It is Well

judgment: blessed are all they that wait for him.

Isaiah 40 v 31 But they that wait upon the LORD shall renew their strength; they shall mount up with wings as eagles; they shall run, and not be weary; and they shall walk, and not faint.

Psalms 27 v 14 Wait on the LORD: be of good courage, and he shall strengthen thine heart: wait, I say, on the LORD.

Psalms 37 v 34 Wait on the LORD, and keep his way, and he shall exalt thee to inherit the land: when the wicked are cut off, thou shalt see it.

Proverbs 20 v 22 Say not thou, I will recompense evil; but wait on the LORD, and he shall save thee.

In the Land of Between, when you're on the road between your before and after, don't give up even when it seems impossible. Breathe it

It is Well

in. Enjoy the journey in all its pain and beauty. You will never pass this way again.

> *Wait on the Lord. Be of good courage... Wait, I say, on the Lord!* (Psalm 27:14)

It is Well

It is Well

PART THREE

Blessed

It is Well

11

DON'T LIE TO ME

(2 Kings 4v8-37)
The Shunamite woman noticed that Elisha the prophet was doing good works every time he came through their community. She persuaded her husband to build a little apartment for the prophet so that whenever he came to the village, he could stay with them. In return, Elisha approached the woman and asked her, "You have taken good care of me and my servant. Is there anything that I can do for you in return?" His servant Gehazi spoke up and said, "She has no son, and her husband is old." And so, Elijah promised her that in a year's time, she would give birth to a son. The only response she had was, "Please don't lie to me!"

It happened as the prophet promised. She conceived and bore a son, who grew and appeared healthy. But one day in the fields with his father, he clutched his head, calling out in pain. Frantically, his father brought the boy back to his mother who held him on her knees, clutched close to her chest. "It will be well, baby. You'll see. Everything will be okay. You're my special gift, my miracle baby. It will be well." She remained like that for hours, cradling and comforting her son until about noon that day, then sadly and without explanation, he died in her arms.

She called for her husband, asked for a donkey, and said, "I need to go see the prophet." When he asked her why she would run out to see him, especially now, she only answered, "It is well." (2 Kings 4 v 26 and 28).

What do you mean, "It is well?"
Heading out on a journey to visit a prophet after a death was not the tradition. In Jewish tradition the deceased must be buried within 24 hours of death, and there is a timeline for things to be completed. "IT IS WELL" is not the anticipated or expected response, nor was mounting a donkey to go find the prophet.

It is Well

People had to be notified, plans needed to be made. Mourners needed to be at her house crying for her lost child. Funeral plans had to be executed within 24 hours of the death. The village of Shunem is approximately 44 km to Mount Carmel by road. On foot, it would have taken almost 9.5 hours to walk there leading a mule bearing a woman and supplies. Seeing as the child died around noon, given the timeline in Jewish tradition for funeral planning, there simply was NO TIME for her to go running off to the mountain of God.

The Shunamite woman's family and friends must have been bewildered at her choice to leave her dead son and to go off on a mission to find the prophet. It is also possible that this woman did not even notify anyone that the boy had died – she simply took him up to the prophet's apartment, laid him on the bed and headed out to find the prophet. Either way, her actions flew in the face of her culture, religion, and tradition. Had her quest to find the prophet resulted in another outcome than the resurrection of her boy, she would have had an awful lot of explaining to do!

It is Well

Sometimes we are going to make choices that are completely based on our faith and trust in God. Others around you, even those closest to you may have questions, may criticize. They won't understand and might try to get you to do what is "expected". But if your instincts tell you to trust in God, do not waver from that!

The woman and her servant rushed to Mount Carmel. Elisha saw her coming and told his servant to go greet her with the question, "Is it well with you, with your husband, with your son?" Her response to Gehazi was, "It is well".

But when she drew near, the prophet could sense her deep despair. She caught him by his feet and said, "Didn't I ask you not to lie to me about the gift of my son?" Immediately, without even knowing all the details, Elijah sensed the urgency of the situation. He sprung into action, with orders for Gehazi to rush ahead of them to the woman's home and see to the child. Elisha remained with her for strength and comfort, but they too headed back home.

It is Well

When they arrived, the child lay still, lifeless and unresponsive, but Elisha lay on the child placed his face over his face, his hands over his hands and the child's blood began to flow again. He did it again, and suddenly the boy started sneezing! Seven times he sneezed and then he opened his eyes (2 Kings 4 v 35).

"Here," he called to the boy's mother. "Pick up your son." Before she rushed to her son, she fell to the prophet's feet, and bowed to the ground in gratitude. Then she embraced her boy (2 Kings 3 v 37).

This woman was blessed beyond measure in the recovery of her son from death. As a "blessed" woman, take note that she asked for nothing except for honesty. She was NOT entitled. She humbly accepted the promise of her son, and she only asked that the prophet always tell her the truth and nothing but the truth.
When her son died, she did not descend into the pits of grief. There was no sackcloth or ashes, no weeping and wailing, no tearing of her garments. Instead, she pulled up her big

girl panties and said, "It is well. I'm going to go see the prophet." Throughout her ordeal, she maintained that all was well even though her heart must have been breaking in two.

Humility and Servanthood

The Shunamite woman's humility shows through from the beginning of the story to the ending. In his commentary on this tale, Richard T. Ritenbaugh[iii] states, "The Shunammite woman is described as "notable" (II Kings 4 v 8), a Hebrew word that can connote wealth, piety, renown or elements of each." It occurs to me that today's culture idolizes wealth and scoffs at piety. To be wealthy today means that you can lord yourself above "the little people", be exempt from the rules of society, and outrun the long hand of the law. Yet, this woman's wealth was not the focus of the story. Her willingness to share her wealth to support the prophet and his servant is how the story begins. She may have been rich, but she was humble.

It is Well

Look at what the scripture has to say about the promises of God to those who are humble in spirit.

2 Chronicles 7 v 14 If my people, which are called by my name, shall humble themselves, and pray, and seek my face, and turn from their wicked ways; then will I hear from heaven, and will forgive their sin, and will heal their land.

Job 22 v 29 When men are cast down, then thou shalt say, "There is lifting up; and he shall save the humble person."

Psalms 9 v 12 When he maketh inquisition for blood, he remembereth them: he forgetteth not the cry of the humble.

Psalms 10 v 17 LORD, thou hast heard the desire of the humble…

Proverbs 29 v 23 A man's pride shall bring him low: but honour shall uphold the humble in spirit.

It is Well

Matthew 23 v 12 And whosoever shall exalt himself shall be abased; and he that shall humble himself shall be exalted.

James 4 v 6 But he giveth more grace. Wherefore he saith, God resisteth the proud, but giveth grace unto the humble.

James 4 v 10 Humble yourselves in the sight of the Lord, and he shall lift you up.

1 Peter 5 v 6 Humble yourselves therefore under the mighty hand of God, that he may exalt you in due time.

The Shunammite woman obviously understood this principle and had seen it play out in her life, that humility was accompanied by blessing. Even when her son lay lifeless on a cot, she maintained her humility.

Furthermore, as Ritenbaugh indicates, her piety was evident, as she set aside a room for Elisha and cared for him whenever he came through Shunem (verses 9-10). She was a consistent keeper of the Sabbath, and when

It is Well

she made mention of her plan to visit the prophet on a working day, her husband did not see it as that out of the ordinary. Her servant nature was a key to her character and her choices. She served by providing for her household and for the prophet. She served by keeping the Sabbath and maintaining the traditions of her faith. She was not out for what she could get, but what she could give. The Shunammite woman's Spirit Needs were at work in her life.

The next character trait that defines the Shunammite woman, and a prevailing theme in the search for blessing, is trust. It occurs to me that the Shunammite woman found it easy to trust the Lord because she was in *relationship* with Him. She served GOD by caring for His prophet. She did not provide shelter and food for Elisha because of what she might gain. She clearly loved, trusted, worshipped and served God long before the prophet came to sojourn at her home, and certainly long before God gave her a son. Is it any wonder then that she was so blessed?

It is Well

As I searched through the Bible for references to the word "trust", I found that the author who used this word the most in his writings was none other than David the Psalmist King. It was no surprise to me then, that amid my trials, I sought out the Psalms. David understood the absolute necessity for and the sweetness that is found in trusting in God. Nevertheless, there are references to the value of trusting in God throughout the Word.

In the book of Ruth, trusting in God was cause for a promise of reward (Ruth 2 v 12) "The LORD recompenses thy work, and a full reward be given thee of the LORD God of Israel, under whose wings thou art come to trust". 2 Samuel 22 v 31 reminds us of the importance of trusting in God: "As for God, his way is perfect; the word of the LORD is tried: he is a buckler to all them that trust in him". These exact words are echoed in Psalms 18 v 30.

Psalms 4 v 5 commands us to trust: "Offer the sacrifices of righteousness and put your trust in the LORD". Psalms 9 v 10 is a promise: "And they that know thy name will put their trust in thee: for thou, LORD, hast not forsaken them that seek thee".

Psalms 18 v 2 declares this affirmation: "The LORD is my rock, and my fortress, and my deliverer; my God, my strength, in whom I will trust; my buckler, and the horn of my salvation, and my high tower".

Psalms 20 v 7 is a declaration of pending victory: "Some trust in chariots, and some in horses: but we will remember the name of the LORD our God".

Psalms 25 v 2 and 20 is a prayer: "O my God, I trust in thee: let me not be ashamed, let not mine enemies triumph over me. O keep my soul, and deliver me: let me not be ashamed; for I put my trust in thee".
Who could pray this way, proclaim a yet unachieved victory, or stress the importance of trusting in God except for those who truly know Him as the God who heals, provides, saves, and delivers?

It is Well

If you want to be truly blessed, get to know the God of your salvation. Put your trust in Him, "and do good; so shalt thou dwell in the land, and verily thou shalt be fed" (Psalms 37 v 3). "Commit thy way unto the LORD; trust also in him; and he shall bring it to pass" (Psalms 37 v 5).

> *I will say of the LORD, He is my refuge and my fortress: my God; in him will I trust. He shall cover thee with his feathers, and under his wings shalt thou trust: his truth shall be thy shield and buckler (Psalms 91 v 2 and 4).*

It is Well

12

Hannah's Song

1 Samuel 1 v 1 begins: Now there was a certain man of Ramathaimzophim, of mount Ephraim, and his name was Elkanah, the son of Jeroham, the son of Elihu, the son of Tohu, the son of Zuph, an Ephrathite. And he had two wives; the name of the one was Hannah, and the name of the other Peninnah: and Peninnah had children, but Hannah had no children.

And this man went up out of his city yearly to worship and to sacrifice unto the LORD of hosts in Shiloh. And the two sons of Eli, Hophni and Phinehas, the priests of the LORD, were there. And when the time was that Elkanah offered, he gave to Peninnah his wife, and to all her sons and her daughters, portions. But unto Hannah he gave a worthy portion; for he loved Hannah: but the LORD had shut up her womb. And her adversary also provoked her sore, for to make her fret, because the LORD had shut up her womb. And as he did so year by year, when she went up to the house of the LORD, so she provoked her; therefore, she wept and did not eat.

Then said Elkanah her husband to her, "Hannah, why weepest thou? and why eatest thou not? and why is thy heart grieved? am not I better to thee than ten sons?"

So, Hannah rose up after they had eaten in Shiloh, and after they had drunk. Now Eli the priest sat upon a seat by a post of the temple of the LORD. And she was in bitterness of soul, and prayed unto the LORD, and wept sore. And she vowed a vow, and said, "O LORD of hosts, if thou wilt indeed look on the affliction of thine handmaid, and remember me, and not forget thine handmaid, but wilt give unto thine handmaid a man child, then I will give him unto the LORD all the days of his life, and there shall no razor come upon his head."

It is Well

...Then Eli answered and said, "Go in peace: and the God of Israel grant thee thy petition that thou hast asked of him." And she said, "Let thine handmaid find grace in thy sight." So, the woman went her way and did eat, and her countenance was no more sad.

And they rose up in the morning early, and worshipped before the LORD, and returned, and came to their house to Ramah: and Elkanah knew Hannah his wife; and the LORD remembered her. Wherefore it came to pass, when the time was come about after Hannah had conceived, that she bare a son, and called his name Samuel, saying, "Because I have asked him of the LORD."

The story continues in 1 Samuel 1 v 26: And she said (to Eli), "Oh my lord, as thy soul liveth, my lord, I am the woman that stood by thee here, praying unto the LORD. For this child I prayed; and the LORD hath given me my petition which I asked of him. Therefore, also I have lent him to the LORD; as long as he liveth he shall be lent to the LORD." And he worshipped the LORD there.

It is Well

Hannah's song of praise
1 Samuel 2 v 1 records Hannah's victory prayer: And Hannah prayed, and said, "My heart rejoiceth in the LORD, mine horn is exalted in the LORD: my mouth is enlarged over mine enemies; because I rejoice in thy salvation. There is none holy as the LORD: for there is none beside thee: neither is there any rock like our God. Talk no more so exceeding proudly; let not arrogancy come out of your mouth: for the LORD is a God of knowledge, and by him actions are weighed.

"The bows of the mighty men are broken, and they that stumbled are girded with strength. They that were full have hired out themselves for bread; and they that were hungry ceased: so that the barren hath born seven; and she that hath many children is waxed feeble.

"The LORD killeth, and maketh alive: he bringeth down to the grave, and bringeth up. The LORD maketh poor, and maketh rich: he bringeth low, and lifteth up. He raiseth up the poor out of the dust, and lifteth up the beggar from the dunghill, to set them among princes, and to make them inherit the throne of glory: for the pillars of the earth are the LORD'S, and he hath set the world upon them.

"He will keep the feet of his saints, and the wicked shall be silent in darkness; for by strength shall no man prevail. The adversaries of the LORD shall be broken to pieces; out of heaven shall he thunder upon them: the LORD shall judge the ends of the earth; and he shall give strength unto his king, and exalt the horn of his anointed."

Hannah's prayer reveals the heart of a mother desperate for uniqueness and love and belonging. She wanted to have a child to fill those needs. But her prayer and resulting response to her miracle reveals the heart of a woman, a mother who understood that all things are in God's control.

"This is how I fight my battles"
I particularly love the final verse in Hannah's song of praise because it reminds us that the Lord will fight our battles for us, and that nothing can stand against the Lord of hosts.

It is Well

My family and I have an affinity for tales of medieval times. My boys grew up fascinated with the films and books of Tolkein's *Lord of the Rings*. Once my husband and I saw the boys' obsession with all things, "battle", we directed them to the Bible and shared with them the stories of the victories of the Children of Israel, and of David's mighty men. We wanted them to know of the strength and power that is ours when we fight in Jesus' name.

Ephesians 6 v 10 - 18 reads: Put on the whole armour of God, that ye may be able to stand against the wiles of the devil. For we wrestle not against flesh and blood, but against principalities, against powers, against the rulers of the darkness of this world, against spiritual wickedness in high places. Wherefore take unto you the whole armour of God, that ye may be able to withstand in the evil day, and having done all, to stand.

Stand therefore, having your loins girt about with truth, and having on the breastplate of righteousness and your feet shod with the preparation of the gospel of peace; above all, taking the shield of faith, wherewith ye shall be able to quench all the fiery darts of the wicked. And take the helmet of salvation, and the sword of the Spirit, which is the word of God: praying always with all prayer and supplication in the Spirit, and watching thereunto with all perseverance and supplication for all saints."

Certainly, you have heard many a sermon preached on the whole armour of God, and I have no intention of trying to best any of those messages; however, there is something here for us mothers – a nugget of truth and wisdom – it is hidden within the section of scripture that speaks of the *shield of faith*. But first, a brief history about shields.

A shield was a multipurpose tool for hunters. It was used dually for defense from an adversarial beast, but also for concealment when stalking one's prey. In other words, while a shield could be used for protection, it also acted as camouflage so one could *sneak up* on one's prey.

It is Well

All my life I have heard that the devil wanders about as a roaring lion, seeking whom he may destroy – that he is the king of the jungle and I am the lowly prey, a helpless gazelle whose only defense is to run. I'm not so sure that is true! If faith is my shield, I can absolutely use it to quench the fiery darts of the enemy, but I can also use my faith as a buffer to get me close enough to inflict a killing blow to that which would bring me harm.

Think of this. Throughout the Greek and then the Roman conquests, shields were an essential tool of warfare. The size and composition of a shield depended entirely on the *tactical* demands of the user. The more effective the armour, the smaller the shield. Likewise, the longer the reach of the weapon (e.g. spear vs. sword), the smaller the shield. We are instructed to put on the WHOLE armour of God – why? So that all the pieces work in concert with the shield. Faith will certainly be a defensive weapon but by itself, it would not be enough. A well-designed breastplate deflects arrows and glances from swords. A strong helmet protects the head from flying arrows, rocks, and other projectiles. Good shoes are an absolute must when in the field of battle. All armour elements that protect the vital organs and the reproductive organs are also necessary. Faith alone cannot protect you. You need truth, a righteous heart and a "heart" knowledge of the gospel, a willingness to share the good news of Christ, the helmet of salvation and the Word of God, which is your sword. All of this must be covered in prayer if you are to be victorious in spiritual battle.

The Greek *hoplon* was a circular shield made of wood and bronze, whereas the Roman *scutum* was a large cylindrical shield designed to cover most of the body. Both shields had offensive properties – they were not just made for defensive tactics. A *scutum* weighed between 10 and 20 lbs, and it was anchored to the left arm of a soldier with leather straps and a handle on the inner side. This helped with managing the weight and assisted the soldier with maneuvering the shield into different positions. The handle was secured with a piece of metal on the exterior, front-facing section of the shield called a *boss*, which, when backed by the strength of a 20 lb shield and the force of the man carrying it, struck a powerful blow against anyone in its way. (This is referred to as "shield bash"). Using a *scutum* offensively would have the effect of punching someone with a "massive set of brass knuckles"[iv].

A *hoplon* also made for a formidable offensive weapon. Smaller and easier to maneuver than the larger, more cumbersome *scutum*, the *hoplon* allowed the user to advance on his enemy, getting up close so that a lethal blow could be made with the sword. Romans used a double-edged sword with an 18-inch blade called a *gladius*. When paired with a *hoplon*, the gladius could wreak maximum damage.

There are times when the nature of your battle calls for the full defense of a *scutum*. *Scuta* were invaluable when a line of infantry was advancing on the enemy. They could break into various formations, enabling complete protection of the line from the front, and from above – quenching the fiery darts of

It is Well

the enemy – by covering the heads and shoulders of their fellow soldiers and themselves. My sisters, there are times when we need to cover ourselves and our sisters with faith. Together, working as a unified body, a single unit moving and advancing against our common enemy, we can be more effective than alone.

There are also times when the *hoplon* must be the shield of choice. When you are clothed in the whole armour of God, your *hoplon* allows you to advance on your enemy while battling him with your *gladius* – the Word of God. As you advance, you can use the blunt or sharp edge of your shield as well as the *boss* to deliver offensive blows that confuse the enemy and set him off balance, allowing you to use your sword to strike.

In my research, I watched a recreation of a man-to-man battle in the form of the ancient Roman *Provocatori*[iv] and realized something else about shields. Having a shield is not enough to keep you protected. If you don't know how to use your shield, you're as good as dead. Your faith cannot be something you just fling about while you hope for the best. A shield is as much a strategic weapon as a sword or a lance. You must be able to anticipate your enemy's attack and be ready to deflect or make an offensive move before your foe can strike.

The other principle of battle I learned as I watched the re-enactment, is that you must NEVER turn your back on your enemy. The shield is for *advancement,* not for retreat. The assumption in battle is that someone has your back. When you are fighting with another, you don't always fight side-by-side; you must also be prepared to fight back to back, to protect each other from an unforeseen attack.

Ladies, the Mom Blunder of denial is so dangerous! While you are burying your head in the sand and hoping your trial will go away if you just ignore it, the battle will rage on around you. Shore up your faith. Put on the whole armour of God and wield your shield of faith with strategy and intention! With it, you can bash your opponent, throw him off balance, and strike with your *gladius.*

Strength in flexibility

The strength of *scuta* was found in their construction. Thin layers of wood were glued on top of each other with alternating patterns of grain. Every second layer of wood was glued down with the grain flowing in a 90-degree angle from the previous layer. This made the wood stronger and more pliable so it could be shaped into its cylindrical form. It is from this ancient method of bonding thin slices of wood that we get the term, "plywood". Here's where it gets interesting. When you bond several layers of wood together with the grain all flowing in the same direction, that wood is easily broken apart when met with a blunt force. The patterned layering makes the wood more flexible and gives it more strength and resistance. Is it not so with our faith? If we keep a narrow perspective of our faith, if we do not stretch it, and allow ourselves to step out in different directions under God's leading, our faith may become brittle and easily broken, as with Elijah's widow woman.

It is Well

But taking each experience and what we learn from it, layering it across the one that came before, essentially weaving together each instance of God's faithfulness in our lives gives us strength, resiliency, flexibility, and resistance against the trials we will face today and in the future.

The Spartans, arguably, the fiercest of Greek warriors had a saying before they went out to battle: "Return with your shield, or on it." In other words, fight for your life – use your shield as your defense and as a tool to help you gain the victory, but if you die, come home on your shield. Take this adage to heart. Whenever we go to battle for ourselves, our family, our church, or your community, we must put on the whole armour of God, and let faith go before us. We must use it to advance our attack on the enemy, to keep him off balance and confused so that with the Word of God, we may strike the killing blow. And when the time comes for us to leave this world for glory, let us do so, still firmly resting on our faith.

13

WHEN CRISIS COMES

It was the spring of 2015, and there was a disturbance deep in my spirit, as though I could sense something bad was coming my way. I attended the Ontario Ladies Conference and listened as Janice Sjostrand spoke directly into my life. I had already been in travail for my son – instinctively, I felt something was wrong. Sister Sjostrand spoke to our ladies' group about real life and real challenges. She had some of the ladies share testimonies of how tragedy or crisis had struck their lives and how they had trusted in God to bring them through.

Then she told us point blank, "Right now, you are all on the mountaintop and you're feeling

It is Well

good. But you are leaving this place to face real life trials. Crises are on their way to you, and you are going to need the strength from this weekend to get you through it." She followed that statement with this: "God may not prevent the coming storm from battering your life, but He WILL give you the grace to get through it. So, *pray for grace.*" I received that word and carried it with me into the oncoming storm.

When tragedy strikes and crisis comes, it would be easy to collapse under the weight of the burden or care. The Word of God has showed us though, that there are ways to overcome the storm itself, and to come through not just bitter or better, but truly **blessed**.

When faith is lacking
Job's wife was too miserable and frankly, too selfish to see that her husband was also suffering. All she could see was what they had lost. She had NO faith in Job's God to restore their joy, their family, or their material possessions. Sometimes in our lives we can

It is Well

be like Mrs. Job – so focused on the things we have lost, that we cannot see what blessings are right in front of us.

When faith is shaky
If you read 1 Kings 7 v 8-17 you will see that the widow started out with great faith, but it would seem her faith was more in the prophet rather than the God he served. When tragedy struck and threatened to take her son away, whatever faith she had before died. Rather than turning to God to be her support, she turned on the prophet, blaming him for her son's death. Only once her son was restored to her did she express faith in God, and it was nothing like the childlike faith she started with in the beginning. She lost her footing when she began to rely on the MAN more than she relied on his God.

When faith is strong
The Shunamite woman knew her son was a GIFT. Can you imagine the anguish she felt as she helplessly held her precious son in her arms until he passed away? Yet, through her grief she was able to say, "IT IS WELL". The

difference-maker for her, as it was for Hannah, was her knowledge of and her faith and trust in the One true God.

It's not your fault
Often when tragedy strikes, as in the case of most of our Biblical examples, IT IS NOT OUR FAULT. We have already established that moms tend to have a lot of guilt but blaming yourselves or others for what happens doesn't help to solve the problem. No matter how deep your grief or sorrow, it is NEVER okay to hurt someone else or to strike out in anger at others. Remember that statement: "Hurt People Hurt People?" That doesn't need to be the case.

Children are a GIFT from God
Psalm 127 v 3 - Children are a heritage of the Lord, and the fruit of the womb is his reward. The best thing we moms could ever do is to entrust them to His care and keeping. Trying to fix their problems ourselves is not the answer, not when we have a God who knows the end from the beginning and is all powerful

and everywhere present. What do we really think we can do that God cannot?

What is in your hand?
Many times, we already have the resources we need for God to work. We can't allow grief to blind us from the blessings we still have, and we might lose out on our miracle if we don't listen when God asks, "What is that in your hand?" The widow in 2 Kings 4 v 1-7 lost her husband. Not her fault. Her late husband's debts? Not her fault. She was directed to a resource she already had but THOUGHT had no value. It was the leveraging of that resource that brought her the miracle that saved her family.

I was watching the Antique Road Show in which a woman brought a unique necklace to be appraised. The necklace was made up of gold, some precious jewels and rare stones. It appeared to be a one-of-a-kind item that had been left to her by her mother, and it had been in the family for a couple of generations.

It is Well

I gasped in horror as the woman related the provenance of the necklace and admitted to the appraiser that she had traded this precious family heirloom with a neighbour for a dog. She insisted the terrier was well-loved and that she did not want the necklace returned. Yet, she was curious enough about the necklace that she borrowed it back from the current owner to bring it to the show and have it appraised.

I recall thinking, *"This woman had better love her dog a WHOLE lot. She traded something that clearly has a high financial and sentimental value for a relationship that may be fulfilling, but at the end of the day, will still be temporal."* Perhaps the terrier's value was about $500. The appraiser estimated the value of the necklace at almost $2000. Too late though: the necklace's value would mean nothing as she had already traded it away.

Oh, that we would not be like this woman. What a shame it would be if we traded away our relationship with God, our trust in Him, our reliance on Him for something that was temporal in nature! Think of the farmer who sold the field so he could purchase a precious gem, but when the field was sold the new owner found the field was rich with natural resources. Too often we are so caught up in our crisis that we do not see what is already in our hand.

If only we could be attentive to the voice of the Lord and pay attention to the blessings already in our midst, so that when He asks, "What is that in your hand?" that we may answer, "Many are the blessings that you have given to me! Show me how to use what You have already provided to meet this present need." Even in her distress, the widow was willing to spring into action, making good use of all the empty vessels she had in her home. What if we could be like her, and make a shift in our perception to see what we once believed to be empty, useless things, as tools through which God might demonstrate His awesome power?

It is Well

You have a choice
When things go wrong, and tragedy strikes your family, you can choose how you will respond. You can become bitter and resentful like Mrs. Job. You can blame your husband, the church or the body of Christ. You can blame the preacher. OR you could be like the Shunamite woman and put your trust in the Lord despite your distress and trust Him that "IT IS WELL". Remember Prov. 3 v 5. *Trust in the Lord with all thine heart and lean not on thine own understanding.* That means, we can't trust our feelings because FEELINGS LIE.

This is a theme that keeps cropping up in my conversations with clients, and church members alike. At our annual Ontario Ladies Conference, a woman approached me and said, "Whenever I want to praise God, I FEEL like the enemy attacks me, and then I stop." I did my best to encourage her, but even after the conversation was over, I turned what she said over and over in my head. Then later that same day, the Lord spoke to me and told me to go and find this woman. I went searching

It is Well

for her in a crowd of about 450 ladies, and just as I was about to give up on the search, she found me.

I pulled her aside, indicating that the Lord had given me a word for her. The word was basically this: praise is not predicated by our feelings. It doesn't matter what the enemy throws at us, or if we FEEL like we are under attack. Feelings lie all the time. If we had to wait until we were feeling just right before we could praise God, I would guess that none of us ever would!

We praise God because of what He has done. And here's the thing: even if God has never done anything that you can readily identify in your life as "miraculous", let's not overlook what He accomplished through creation, or the work that was finished by Christ on the cross. Consider that Christ saw you still in your sin, and He chose to go to the cross as a sacrifice for you. Is that not enough for us to praise Him?

It is Well

Think about the fact that He trades with us beauty for ashes. Think of all the many ways in which we can praise Him. The ebb and flow of the winds and waves, the gentle swaying of tree branches, the chirping of birds, the beauty in a butterfly's wings all exist to give glory to God. Surely, we can raise our hands, sing praise, or if we don't have energy for that, we can make melody in our hearts to the Lord (Ephesians 5 v 19). Praise can be a joyful noise, but it doesn't have to be. Praise is an acknowledgement of all that God has done and HOW you do that is up to you.

Why do we trust feelings as truth? The Bible declares that the Word of God is truth. It also admonishes us to NOT trust our feelings. When your feelings tell you that all hope is lost, that you are unworthy, that you might as well give up, that nothing good can come from your efforts and hard work; when they tell you to be anxious and afraid, to wallow in depression; when they tell you that no-one cares about you and that you are alone in your suffering, remind yourself that feelings lie.

I think of Job's wife and the feelings she must have allowed to consume her in the days following the deaths of her children. Without faith in Job's God to sustain her, I can see how she must have wallowed in those feelings that told her, "all hope is lost. The legacy we built has been destroyed. There will be no one to care for us in our old age. We can never recover from this." Can you see how when left unchecked, these feelings and erroneous beliefs might drive her to a place of bitterness and rage?

Faith and Trust

There are two recurring themes that present themselves frequently throughout this study. They are faith and trust. You might wonder, aren't faith and trust the same thing? I thought so too, at first, but then as I delved deeper into this study, I began to make a distinction between the two words and how they are played out in real life.

Faith is defined as, "a strong belief based on spiritual apprehension rather than proof", "complete trust or confidence in someone or something".[vi]

When I think of the word, "faith", I think of the scripture that says that those who come to God must *believe* that He is. I think also of the fact that the demons believe in God and they tremble. Faith in God – believing that *He is,* is a good start but it isn't enough. If so, the demons would have the potential to be redeemed simply because of their faith in God. No, there must be more.

Trust is "a firm belief in the reliability, truth, ability, or strength of someone or something. Confidence, conviction, reliance, assurance. To believe that a person or thing is good, truthful or strong. To hope. To allow someone to look after something or to use it on your behalf. To accept the truth of a statement without evidence or investigation."[vii]

While Faith might be believing in something, we can only conceive of but haven't yet seen, trust is an EXTENSION of faith. Some are starting out with no God consciousness – no real convictions one way or the other that God exists and that He is a rewarder of them that diligently seek Him. Others have that God consciousness, but they do not believe that God is interested in their lives, nor have they cultivated any kind of relationship with Him. That kind of faith is conceptual, but *trust* is the act of extending ourselves further and believing with conviction that God not only IS, but that He will do what He has promised to do.

When we trust in God, we are in effect, **demonstrating** our faith in Him. Remember this: faith without works is dead. Trusting God is an ACT or a work of FAITH. When we trust God, we are in effect acting on our belief in His reliability, truth, ability and strength. We are demonstrating our belief that He is good, truthful, and strong. We are putting our hope in Him, and we place our lives and our children into His hands to look after them on our behalf. When we trust God, we accept the truth of His word without evidence!

It is Well

Can you do that today? Can you put your trust in a loving God who knows the number of hairs on your head; the same God who sees every sparrow that falls; will you put your life into His hands and entrust the keeping of your family to Him?

I heard recently that **"if you only serve and trust in God during the good times, then you don't really LOVE Him, you're just USING Him."** To be able to say, IT IS WELL during times of crisis demonstrates our faith in God and His promises. That doesn't mean that as mothers, we won't be anxious for our children, but we have an anchor, an assurance that if we have committed our kids back to the Lord, then we can trust that His perfect will is what will happen in their lives.

It is Well

14

WHEN YOUR DAUGHTER IS VIOLATED

*[*The names and some of the details of this true story have been altered to protect the anonymity of the subjects. The name Camilla means, "perfect; virgin of unblemished character" and the name Valerie means, "strong or valiant".]*

It seemed innocent enough. Spend the night at your best friend's house with some other girls. There's safety in numbers, right? Be sure to stay with your friends, and don't allow yourself to be found alone with the man of the house. 13-year-old Camilla* knew these rules and followed them to the letter. But on the day Camilla stopped by her friend's house to say hello, she did not realize her friend was

It is Well

not at home; instead, she was out of town visiting her mom. Her friend's father was "the cool dad". Everyone liked him. He told her to wait for her friend who would be up from the basement in a few minutes. Once he had her in the house, he sexually assaulted her, threatening her with a weapon that she was to tell no one what had happened.

Camilla's mom, Valerie noticed Camilla started taking long showers and very hot baths. Valerie's husband had noticed that some of the warning signs as well: Camilla was throwing up a lot, she wasn't sleeping, keeping her light on at night, needed her doors and windows closed, and would listen to Bible tapes all night long. If Valerie turned the Bible tapes off, Camilla would wake up immediately – it was like she needed it to feel safe at night.

Maybe it was just a teenage girl thing. But when Camilla fell ill several days later, her mother rushed her to the doctor. What could it be? A virus? Food poisoning? When the doctor asked her to leave the examination room so she could speak with Camilla alone, Valerie knew something was dreadfully wrong.

Valerie recalls those moments surrounding finding out what had happened to her daughter. She says, "I was overwhelmed with two emotions: compassion and shock. I remember I was at once trying to process her pain and my pain. I'm her mother – I was supposed to keep her safe from that! I felt like a failure because I didn't keep her safe."

On that fateful day that all was revealed, Valerie recalls that she had gone out for a walk, leaving Camilla home with her brother. He called Valerie to say Camilla was very sick, and to come home right away. She rushed home and went to a walk-in clinic right away. They checked Camilla and supposed she had strep throat maybe from throwing up. They encouraged Valerie to book an appointment with the doctor. They did.

Valerie remembers Camilla did not want her to accompany her to the doctor, which was

It is Well

unusual. "When the doctor came out, she was looking at me like she felt sorry for me. I didn't understand what was happening." Valerie soon made sense of the doctor's response, when she saw that she had requisitioned immediate blood testing and realized they were testing Camilla for pregnancy.

Camilla started to cry and said she didn't want to talk about why she was pregnant; however, she eventually told her mother what happened. "I held her hand all the way while she told the story in the car," Valerie says. They had found out afterwards, that only a week earlier another of Camilla's friends had been raped by the same man at a sleepover.

Camilla decided to keep the baby. For this incredibly courageous decision, she was ridiculed by her peers, shunned by her teachers, and shamed by the ministry. Meanwhile, the perpetrator of the crime was charged and tried. After two mistrials, finally the man was convicted and sentenced. Those are the facts of the story. We could leave it there, but can we even begin to understand what it must have been like for Valerie during this time?

Valerie shared with me the emotions she experienced as she walked through the fire with Camilla. Fear was at times overwhelming. She remembered feeling anger and frustration and fear for her daughter. After finding out what happened, Valerie and her husband called the police right away – also called their pastor, who came over right away.
"We had to think about school and what Camilla was going to go through there. As it turns out, they banished her; they were ashamed to have her. She was in grade 8 and wanted to go to graduation, but it was an embarrassment for them. The girls at school started bullying her, calling her a liar, and threatening to beat her up." Therefore, Valerie turned to home schooling.

"People started throwing things at us and pressuring us to make a decision. Nothing was left off the table from abortion to adoption. Camilla knew she had to live with whatever she decided. Valerie reassured her that they would stand with her no matter what.

The family's church was very uncomfortable with what had happened. Someone suggested having a baby shower for young Camilla. But hosting a baby shower for a child of rape? It hurt to know that the church thought about what might be more embarrassing for the ladies of the church rather than doing right by a hurting girl.

Valerie admits that she lost a lot of friends over this trial. Her well-intentioned Christian friends, like Job's friends gave poor counsel – advising them to have Camilla give the baby up for adoption. Valerie says this hurt most of all. People were more worried about the "shame" of what had happened (as though it were somehow Camilla's fault) and did not think about that unborn child's future. They did not consider what his best chance at life would look like. Valerie remembers arguing against adoption: "He wasn't just a child of rape, he was *ours* – our flesh and blood!"

It is Well

"We challenged everyone who advised us to have him placed in a stranger's home – if they could guarantee that a stranger would love him more than us, and that a stranger would ensure that he was raised in the church with a heart to love and serve God, then we would give him up. Of course, no one could make such a guarantee. We told them, 'We will love him and raise him right, and raise him in the church. He will never go a single day without knowing that he is loved and wanted'."

Valerie and her husband did something amazing for their daughter: they had themselves listed as his parents along with her. When they made the commitment to love and raise their grandson, they made it legal. They raised him for 8 years, and he has been a vital part of their lives.

Valerie recalls that when they sat with the court appointed counsellor, and Camilla had to tell her everything, Valerie wept the whole time. She couldn't help feeling that her daughter's childhood had been stolen from her. Looking back now, the family sees

It is Well

Camilla's son as a treasure and a gift from God. "The name we gave him means, 'laughter'," says Valerie. "He is aptly named – he brings such joy and laughter into our lives."

As I interviewed Valerie, I had so many questions. What was the most difficult part of this crisis? How did she find strength throughout the ordeal? What scriptures did she depend on? How did she work through the feelings of bitterness so that she could become better and eventually blessed? Here is what she shared with me.

<u>Praise</u> is what got me through it.
"Every time we went to church, we worshipped hard and praised through it. We had a strong foundation, a solid prayer life, and a strong relationship with God – without that these things will shake you. When our kids backslid and walked away from God, we wanted them always to know that our home was a safe place, and that we always worshipped and served God. And our son has told us that is why he serves God today

It is Well

because his parents were an example for him. If we had left the church, he wouldn't have found his way back."

What is the TRUTH that Valerie learned or solidified through this trial? What did she learn about friendship, about faith, about family, about failure, and about fortitude?

Valerie says, "Trials challenge your faith in God. You have to believe HARDER – that God has a purpose and a reason for everything." The foundation of Valerie's faith is what kept her through it all.

I asked Valerie what values she tried to instill in Camilla. Valerie's primary focus was for her daughter to maintain consistency in her walk with God and to trust that He would keep her through everything. She recalls, "I kept reminding her that she could never lose her faith in God. Once she said to me, 'Mom, I have no faith in God anymore.' I replied to her, 'Don't you ever say that again! God did not do this to you, but He will help you get through this.'" Today, Valerie says even

It is Well

though her daughter is not in right relationship with God, she still has faith in Him, and she has never forgotten what her mother taught her.

Another thing Valerie did was to consistently take her daughter to church. When she was depressed, when her belly was swollen with child, in the early years when she used drugs to self-medicate and to numb the pain of her trauma, her mom brought her to church. Not only did Valerie ensure her daughter was in God's house, but she worshipped with enthusiasm so her children would always see that her love for God was not contingent on her circumstances.

Valerie stood by her daughter through every aspect of her ordeal. She was there for every doctor's appointment, took her to therapy, attended every court session, and walked with her everywhere they went. When they went out together, she would hold her daughter's hand when people stared at her. She slept in Camilla's bed with her when she had nightmares. Even when it came time for the baby to be delivered, Valerie and her husband were right there with their daughter.

"Vengeance is mine", says the Lord

As Valerie and I discussed the many painful aspects of this experience, we eventually fell on the question – "Didn't you ever want to take revenge? Would it not have been satisfying to punish that man yourself rather than go through the agony of three trials? Again, Valerie shook her head, and replied, "We didn't want to take things into our own hands, because we had left them in God's hands and with the courts," Valerie says of their decision to let God be in control. "We didn't want Camilla to feel more guilt or to blame herself if her father did something to punish the man that raped her and then ended up in jail as a result."

When I asked Valerie *how* she was able to leave this situation in God's hands, her answer came quick and easy. "Prayer," she said. "I hit my knees knowing that no matter what, I needed to be strong for my daughter, and I trusted God to fight her battles for her."

It is Well

Valerie's advice to hurting travailing moms is simple.
- Take it one day at a time
- Go to church. Be consistent in your worship. Love God no matter what.
- Do not feel guilty for your anger or when you want to do something that "is not spiritual". Turn those feelings over to God and allow yourself to be human. Valerie mentioned that whenever she felt like taking matters into her own hands, she would worship more and pour her heart out to God.
- Let people go who try to speak "wisdom" into your life, who are only seeking to serve themselves. Ask God for discernment to know the difference between those who speak for Him and those who do not.

Consistency is Key

One of the most valuable things I learned from my conversation with Valerie is the importance of maintaining consistency on behalf of your children. From the very beginning of their ordeal, Valerie and her husband thought about the impact of their actions and reactions and how the decisions they made in the moment would affect the lives of their children and their grandchildren for the long term.

When people told them that the child should be given up for adoption, their response was, "Promise us that whoever adopts this child will raise him to love and serve God like we would." When no guarantees could be given, the choice was clear. They would raise their grandson in the fear and admonition of the Lord, and he would always know that he was wanted and that he was loved. Many years later when they sat down with their boy to explain his origins, they asked him if he ever felt unloved in their home, and he said, "absolutely never". He had never felt he didn't belong, or that he wasn't part of the family.

Standing on His Promises
Valerie shared a few key scriptures that carried her through her family's crisis. She noted that Philippians 4 v 13, "I can do all things through Christ who strengthens me"

was a verse she returned to often. She also quoted Psalms 18 v 2 "The LORD is my rock, and my fortress, and my deliverer; my God, my strength, in whom I will trust; my buckler, and the horn of my salvation, and my high tower", and Psalm 91 v 2, "I will say of the LORD, He is my refuge and my fortress: my God; in him will I trust."

Finally, a few weeks after our interview, she approached me with yet another scripture that she said often helped her through many a dark night: 1 Peter 4 v 12, which says, "Beloved, think it not strange concerning the fiery trial which is to try you, as though some strange thing happened unto you: but rejoice, inasmuch as ye are partakers of Christ's sufferings; that, when his glory shall be revealed, ye may be glad also with exceeding joy."

Ministry Impact
Valerie says that her and her husband's ministry is centered in helping people who are hurting, bringing healing and restoration into people's lives. She says that they both agree

that God allowed those events to take place in their lives to prepare them for their ministry.

"Not for one second do I regret having my grandson in our lives," she says. "He brings us so much joy."

When I asked Valerie about the **mom blunders** and how they evidenced themselves in her life, she said this of blaming the leadership, "When you're that low, you're looking for an outlet and wanting someone SAFE to blame. You must understand that what you expect from the ministry is not always what you're going to get."

Valerie made the distinction between being angry at the ministry and blaming them. She noted that while she and her husband were upset with some of the advice given them, they never blamed the ministry as though what happened was their fault. She did say that they often wrestled with God, frequently asking, "WHY". Here's the thing. God doesn't mind if we wrestle with Him. Jacob did that and was blessed. He doesn't get angry if we negotiate with Him. Abraham did that and saw his nephew saved from destruction. God doesn't mind if we argue with Him! Moses did that and is still considered one of the greatest leaders in history – AND, he is one of the few Biblical characters whose encounters with God left Him permanently and physically changed. What God does not want, is for us to lose our faith and trust in Him. "I could not allow my pain to become my life story," recounts Valerie. "My pain has become my testimony," and now helping hurting people has become her lifelong ministry.

Finally, I asked Valerie what she is still trusting God for. Without hesitation, she said that she is trusting God for her daughter and grandson to live healthy, vibrant lives. She prays that they will live for God and their lives will give Him glory. She hopes that one day soon, their pain will become their testimony and that they will lift others with their story.

God allowed these events to take place in their lives

It is Well

to prepare them for their ministry.

Valerie and her husband are dedicated to creating a culture where ANYONE can be used of God. Their mission is to pour into people's lives, invest in them and give them a vision of how they can contribute. Their family's trial, and their pain has truly become their testimony. It has not only shaped their ministry, but it has defined their legacy.

It is Well

15

WHEN YOUR SON IS IN A COMA

On Friday October 12, 2018, Braidyn Milton left home for school with a friend. It was like any other day – his friend picked him up and they headed out. At 8:04 am, the vehicle carrying Braidyn was involved in a motor vehicle accident that could have taken his life. The vehicle Braidyn was in was hit by a truck going through an intersection, rolled over and Braidyn was thrown into a ditch. He sustained a diffuse axonal injury and was transported by helicopter to Sunnybrook Hospital where he lay in a coma for several weeks. The type of injury Braidyn sustained was one from which 90% of people who have this injury never recover. 10% of all people who sustain this type of injury, which is the most common AND most serious type of TBI remain in a vegetative state. But his mother

It is Well

never allowed doubt to seep into her life, even though there were some dark days.

Shannon recalls that Braidyn was in an induced coma, while the doctors waited for the swelling in his brain to subside. Some days they were restricted even from touching him, because the stimulation that would cause might activate too much brain activity. She and her husband sat in the trauma center waiting for up to 16 hours a day. Those early weeks were rife with progress and setbacks, but soon signs began to emerge that God was doing a miraculous work in Braidyn's brain. Soon, he began breathing on his own, then responding to commands, **then** spontaneously dropping his leg off his gurney and lifting it back up again. Finally, his eyes opened, and even before he recovered his voice, he was back on his phone, texting his friends!

As the owner of an internet clothing business, Shannon has quite a following on social media. She is no stranger to live streams and posts about clothing, life, and faith. **Hence,** it was no surprise that Shannon documented every step of Braidyn's miraculous recovery with live video and social media posts to her followers. Braidyn's story soon became viral, attracting attention from the local and then regional media. His recovery and the testimony of God's faithfulness is reaching far and wide – an unlikely result from what could have been the ultimate tragedy. One thing I've learned though, is that God likes to work like that! He can take a situation that seems completely hopeless and use it for His glory.

The following testimony is adapted from a post she made in January of this year. When I read it, it pricked my heart. I was not only awed by her transparency, but also her unwavering faith in God throughout the ordeal of Braidyn's recovery. In fact, she told me later that they had just learned of the accident; Trevor was in the helicopter with his son, and she went by car to Sunnybrook. While on her way to the hospital, she had the urge to call an evangelist in her church to request prayer, but then God checked her spirit, essentially prompting her to put her faith in Him and only Him in those first few harrowing hours.

The following, in Shannon's own words, is a testament to what happens when we pray for God to change our hearts, and trust Him to do the work, no matter how painful that process of change might be.

"Lord, Change My Heart"
When the OPP came to tell Trevor and I, and they continued to say we needed to hurry because the accident was bad, my heart sunk. I started to cry. How can this be? He was just going to school! WAIT! Does he know that I love him??

Let's rewind to January 2018. My husband was preaching in Asia, and I was home with the boys. Our church did a week of prayer fasting that week. My personal fast was for a couple of things, the main one being for God to change my heart.

It is Well

Once I finished my fast, I noticed a few changes in other areas. The changing of my heart would come later, I figured.

I am not Braidyn's biological mother. While I have been the mother-figure in his life for the last 13 years, I did not give birth to him. Nine months after I married his father, Children's Aid gave him to us. I was scared and not ready to raise a child, let alone someone else's! **Trevor** was building his company, and I was working full time. Suddenly, I had to make all the changes that were needed to accommodate a child that we previously only had on weekends, so he could be with us full time.

From the time Braidyn was 5 years old, I tickled his back at night, I taught him to read, I showed him how to tie his shoes, picked him up when he fell, wiped away tears, read him stories, cleaned up his vomit, met his teachers, took him for his appointments, took him to get his license, I have had deep **talks** with him and a ton of other things that a mom does.

It is Well

What I DID NOT do, was tell him I love him every day. I didn't always let him "just be a kid", and some days I was really hard on him! 13 years later, we still have Braidyn full time. Full, sole custody. The life we gave him is the only life he knows.

The teenage years have been the hardest for me. Mainly because I didn't feel mature enough to raise a teenager. Still, things had been good at home in the weeks prior to his accident. Two weeks before Braidyn's accident, I saw him sitting off to my left side in church. I looked at him and thought, "Wow. Could it be that my heart hasn't changed? Why is it so hard for me to tell Braidyn I love him? Do I love him like my own? Does he think I love him? Do I?"

I truly felt a nudge in my heart from God. That nudge revealed to me that this was where my heart needed to change the most. How can my heart be changed forever and Braidyn possibly believe that I don't love him? That day, that VERY day, I prayed a prayer at the altar. "God, whatever it takes, WHATEVER it takes!

It is Well

Change my heart." Ladies do not pray this unless you are ready to truly allow God to work in your life. You must be ready to put every ounce of faith you have in HIM!

Twelve days after I prayed that prayer, Braidyn got into his accident.

The first few days following Braidyn's accident, I was totally convinced that I had enough faith that Braidyn would be raised up within three days. I know I did. I knew God was able to do this! Still, God checked my spirit. He told me that this was not MY miracle. This was going to be BRAIDYN'S miracle. This miracle was going to effect and change so many people, Braidyn and I included.

Joseph was not Jesus' biological father. Joseph was His stepfather. While the Bible doesn't say a lot about it, we know that it must've been hard for him to be a father sometimes! Having a pregnant fiancé, knowing that the baby was not his own. Even with an angel coming to him to confirm God's word, I'm sure he doubted sometimes!

It is Well

During the times I was struggling while raising Braidyn, I prayed one prayer over and over. My prayer was simple: "God, give me the love and strength Joseph would have needed to be your father!" You cannot imagine the many tears I shed for this.

One day while sitting there at Sunnybrook, the full measure of my love for Braidyn hit me. I had woken up crying every day since the accident. I realized a piece of me was missing. My heart ached more than it did when my mother killed herself! It hurt so much. I couldn't leave him. I couldn't even think! I had to be there for my boy!

I couldn't leave the hospital. I could not conceive of a life without him. I refused to consider it. He is the older brothers to my boys; he has grown to be my friend.

I am not ashamed to let everyone know that I was not perfect and at times I was so far from it. I made many mistakes and I didn't even take responsibility for them most of the time,

It is Well

until I finally realized that if I want to change, I must first take responsibility for my faults.

Braidyn is my son. I am his Mother, and I will not settle for the title of "step-mom". I have always been Braidyn's mom. He has always made me proud. I have always loved him. I will always love him. I will be the grandmother of his babies. I will be at his wedding (Lord willing) - you get my point, right?

I would not have prayed, behaved or done anything differently if this accident involved one of our other children. I have 3 sons. I love them all with all my heart.

I am so thankful for a merciful God. With my mother, I didn't get a second chance, but with Braidyn I do. I have always been there for him and I always will until I cannot be.

I love, even if it means I will get hurt. I forgive people who have hurt me, and I have asked forgiveness from those whom I have hurt when I was aware. I will continue to say, "I'm sorry." God has given me the strength to make it

It is Well

through all of this. The biggest change started in me. I am still grateful, beyond words for my church and the body of Christ!!

I want to know God and have a relationship with Him. I want to please Him and be pleasing to Him! I don't want religion. I want God living in me and shining from me. Thank you, Jesus for my second chance. Thank you for a Psalm 51 changing of my heart. Changing my heart of stone, into a heart of flesh.

My heart is forever changed!

Psalm 51 King James Version (KJV)
Have mercy upon me, O God, according to thy lovingkindness: according unto the multitude of thy tender mercies blot out my transgressions. Wash me thoroughly from mine iniquity and cleanse me from my sin. For I acknowledge my transgressions: and my sin is ever before me.

Against thee, thee only, have I sinned, and done this evil in thy sight: that thou mightest be justified when thou speakest, and be clear

It is Well

when thou judgest. Behold, I was shapen in iniquity; and in sin did my mother conceive me. Behold, thou desirest truth in the inward parts: and in the hidden part thou shalt make me to know wisdom. Purge me with hyssop, and I shall be clean: wash me, and I shall be whiter than snow.

Make me to hear joy and gladness; that the bones which thou hast broken may rejoice. Hide thy face from my sins, and blot out all mine iniquities. Create in me a clean heart, O God; and renew a right spirit within me. Cast me not away from thy presence; and take not thy holy spirit from me. Restore unto me the joy of thy salvation; and uphold me with thy free spirit. Then will I teach transgressors thy ways; and sinners shall be converted unto thee.

Deliver me from blood guiltiness, O God, thou God of my salvation: and my tongue shall sing aloud of thy righteousness. O Lord open thou my lips; and my mouth shall shew forth thy praise. For thou desirest not sacrifice; else would I give it: thou delightest not in burnt offering. The sacrifices of God are a broken spirit: a broken and a contrite heart, O God, thou wilt not despise.

Lasting Lessons
I asked Shannon if she ever felt the urge to complain, to blame others, or to blame herself for what happened. She replied, "Fortunately, we did not ever have these urges. We did not ever want to see two boy's (the boy who was driving, and Braidyn's) lives ruined! We believe the accident was allowed by God. We aren't the "blaming" type. Perhaps if circumstances were different, we would have struggled with blaming ourselves, but in this case that did not happen."

Blaming church folk or church leadership was not an issue for Shannon either, although, she acknowledged that some people tried to repeatedly speak into her life as though they had a word from the Lord, but when she tested them against what she knew of her situation and of what God had already promised her and Trevor, she recognized that those messages were perhaps more judgement-based than God-inspired. In fact, after discussing one such incident with her husband, he commented, "Remember when the prophet Eli thought Hannah was drunk?" They realized that just because someone spoke into their lives, it did not mean they were doing so on God's behalf. She re-iterated the sentiment already mentioned in Chapter 9 – not everyone has the authority to speak into your life! She suggested the following for those wanting to speak encouragement to moms in crisis. Before you speak:

1. Have you prayed about it?
2. Have you been checked in your spirit to "give advice"?
3. Is it true?
4. Is it kind?
5. Is the "word" you have to offer serving others or is it serving you? Does it imply judgement or is the advice unsolicited?
6. Do you have the right to speak into that mom's life?

"Moms need words of encouragement, prayer, moral and spiritual support," says Shannon. "We had so much of this! People in our church were there for us, but even people we didn't even know reached out to us to let us know they were praying for us." As Shannon and I chatted further about her situation and mine, we agreed that moms in crisis need more than a casserole dropped off at the house. They don't need to be told what they should have been done. They also don't need people who will scoff at their decisions that were made in faith.

"When Jairus's daughter died, Jesus spoke into the parents' lives in front of an audience and they laughed him to scorn. Then He. Kicked. Them. Out." Shannon says emphatically. "If you're going to scorn others in your church family, you best just get out of the way so God can do what He plans without your interference."

Looking to the Future
In one of Shannon's social media posts, I remember her saying, "I don't want to look back on this time in our lives and have to repent, to tell God, 'I'm sorry that I didn't trust

you!' I knew we were in this for the long game."

The answer to prayer for God to change Shannon's heart was a painful one, still Braidyn's accident and his miraculous recovery were conduits to the meeting of Shannon's Spirit Needs. Waiting for God's intervention was an opportunity for growth. Shannon reads her Bible and prays more than she ever did before. She learned through this crisis to lean heavily on the everlasting arms of our Lord, and her faith is stronger than ever. Because of Braidyn's influence in his school and through his football team, his story was spread far and wide. Shannon's experience and her widening sphere of influence has now evolved into a platform through which she can contribute so much encouragement, prayer, and a strong witness of God's miraculous hand and his great faithfulness.

When asked what she would say to moms who fall victim to the Mom Blunders, Shannon noted that she would say,

"Remember this is all about the child fighting for his or her life, not about you. Blaming others won't help your child or you. It won't help anyone. You NEED to stay focused on what's happing now. So, pray. Pray with everything in you and don't lose faith."

Shannon says that her takeaway from this trial is the knowledge that God has gifted her with faith, and with a testimony that is reaching far beyond what she could have ever expected. *"I know I have the gift of faith. It is in me. I believe faith comes from being real! Even though faith is said to be the evidence of things hoped for and not seen, you must be real. Real is when I received the Holy Ghost. Real is when I FELT God with me, although I didn't see Him. REAL is demonstrated in the "coincidences" where God showed Himself to me. Trevor and I had a promise. It was real, and we held onto that. We learned that we must always be open and transparent with God.*

"God used Braidyn's injury and his recovery to touch an entire community of people. Everyone

was reading my posts, so I decided to hold God accountable to both the believer AND the unbeliever. He was not going to let me down. Through that, I've gained the trust of a much larger community. I now use that as a platform to blog and minister."

Shannon relied on several scriptures that carried her through the long days of Braidyn's induced coma and his subsequent recovery.

Jeremiah 32 v 37 Behold, I will gather them out of all countries, wither I have driven them in mine anger, and in my fury, and in great wrath; and I will bring them again unto this place, and I will cause them to dwell safely.

Psalms 91 v 1 and 15 He that dwelleth in the secret place of the most High shall abide under the shadow of the Almighty. He shall call upon me, and I will answer him: I will be with him in trouble; I will deliver him, and honour him.

Ecclesiastes 11 v 5 As thou knowest not what is the way of the spirit, nor how the bones do

It is Well

grow in the womb of her that is with child: even so thou knowest the works of God who maketh all.

2 Corinthians 1 v 20 For all the promises of God in him are yea, and in him Amen, unto the glory of God by us.

Lamentations 3 v 23-26 They are new every morning: great is thy faithfulness. The Lord is my portion, saith my soul; therefore, will I hope in him. The Lord is good unto them that wait for him, to the soul that seeketh him. It is good that a man should both hope and quietly wait for the salvation of the Lord.

Isaiah 65 v 24 And it shall come to pass, that before they call, I will answer; and while they are yet speaking, I will hear.

1 Chronicles 29 v 11 Thine, O Lord, is the greatness, and the power, and the glory, and the victory, and the majesty: for all that is in the heaven and in the earth is thine; thine is the kingdom, O Lord, and thou art exalted as head above all.

It is Well

Mark 11 v 22-24 "Have faith in God. For verily I say unto you, that whosever shall say unto this mountain, be thou removed, and be thou cast into the sea; and shall not doubt in his heart but shall believe that those things which he saith shall come to pass; he shall have whatsoever he saith. Therefore, I say unto you, what things soever ye desire, when ye pray, believe that ye receive them, and ye shall have them."

What I love about the verses Shannon has shared here, is that they are in many ways, a reflection of how we should pray.

Thanksgiving and praise.
Prayer and supplication with faith.
Repentance.
Forgiveness.
Waiting on the Lord for His Word and His provision.

As I read through each of these verses and reflect on them within the context of her experience, I am again reminded of the importance of relying on the Word of God for support and reassurance in difficult times. Even if a Mom Blunder of guilt, shame and self-blame were to invade one's thoughts, or if one might wonder if this trial was just punishment from God, Jeremiah 32 v 37 is a promise that God will return from anger, wrath, and fury, and bring his people again to a place of safety. Worrying that your prayers are hitting the ceiling and bouncing back to you? Trust in Isaiah 65 v 24: Even before you call out to God, He answers, and while you are yet speaking, He will hear you. Feeling abandoned by God? Run to Lamentations 3 and Mark 11. Have faith in God! Remember His mercies are new every morning. **Great is His faithfulness!**

It is Well

16
When Your Child's Future is at Stake

On March 24, 1994 God blessed me with two healthy baby boys. I remember the day I learned I was pregnant with twins. I thought I was miscarrying, and so an emergency ultrasound was ordered. I remember feeling so nervous – on tenterhooks! Then the ultrasound tech showed me what looked like two little vibrating kidney beans on the screen. It took me a moment or two to realize that I was seeing the hearts of two healthy fetuses. I was so relieved, that I started to laugh and couldn't stop. I'm sure the tech thought I was crazy. I was just grateful, shocked but grateful!

It is Well

When my babies came into the world, it was not without drama. I had been scheduled for a C-Section, but the boys had different ideas. After about 25 ½ hours of labour, Dylan came naturally; he was screaming and peeing his way into the world. Then as the doctors began to prepare for the second birth, a quick internal exam revealed a problem.

While Dylan had been pushing his way to freedom, the placenta for my second baby had dropped into the birth canal. Placenta previa is a life-threatening condition for a baby, and so an emergency C-Section was ordered. It was the only way my baby would be born alive. Given that my water had broken over 24 hours prior, my little man was in distress and they needed to get him out as soon as possible. I don't remember much, but I remember my husband standing beside me just repeating over and over, "In Jesus' Name. In Jesus' Name."

Little Thomas was born about 40 minutes later, and after a tense few moments of

It is Well

pumping his little chest and commanding him to breathe, the doctors got my baby breathing and wailing, and shuffled him off to the NICU with his brother. I have never forgotten that day, nor have I ever stopped giving God gratitude for gifting me with two healthy babies. When we had them dedicated to the Lord, I remember praying to God and saying to Him, "You have gifted me with these babies, but they are YOURS. I'm entrusting them to Your care."

My babies' childhood and youth were not without incident, but we made it over each hurdle as a family. The real challenge came after Tom moved away. Towards the end of his second year away from home, in 2015 he sustained a head injury and things began to change. Before that, he had struggled a bit with feelings of loneliness, missing his family, adjusting to being on his own. As his mom, and because I was working in the same city in which he lived, I made efforts to see him every week and to make sure his needs were taken care of.

It is Well

But toward the end of that second year away from home, after the head injury, his personality changed. He became very depressed and started saying he didn't want to come home for holidays. I knew then, that something was wrong. Tom always wanted to be with family during the holidays.

He stayed away that Easter, and it nearly broke me. His lease was up, and he couldn't find a place to stay, so my husband and I encouraged him to just move home. He did, but even then, we could tell something was not quite right. He was getting heavy nosebleeds that wouldn't stop. He didn't tell us that those nosebleeds were often prefaced by bouts of anxiety and uncontrollable crying. He sometimes missed attending church with us because he couldn't make it out of the bathroom in time due to the bleeding. He spent a lot of time on his phone texting his friends and his girlfriend, and he seemed fixated on certain activities. It wasn't until after the 2015 Ladies Conference, about 2 months after he had moved home, that he came to us and told us he was struggling with anxiety and depression, and he thought perhaps he needed help.

We immediately got him to a doctor who prescribed anti-depressant medication. Shortly after that, before the medications could begin to take hold, he left home to stay with friends overnight. That night extended to a week and he did not have enough medication for that time. I begged him to come home, but he kept stalling. By the end of the week, I was in full, "Do it myself" mode, and had decided if he didn't come home, I was going to go get him. I corralled his brother and his sister, and we high-tailed it to Toronto as fast as Dylan's wheels could take us.

But it was too late. While we were in the car on our way, we received a call saying Tom had been arrested for a simple assault. By the time we arrived at the police station, one slap to the face (wrong as it was) had suddenly been inflated to a variety of charges – and the police refused to release him.

It is Well

As a mom, I was terrified. First, because I knew in my heart of hearts that my boy must have been in deep distress to strike out and hit another person. He was the *defender* of the underdog – he was not typically the aggressor. I knew that something had to be truly wrong. Secondly, I feared for my son's safety if he were held in a cell overnight. I know that sounds a little paranoid, but no matter what anyone would like to think, things are different for Black and Indigenous men within the justice system than they are for those who are not racialized. I expressed my fears to the officers, and I explained that my son was having some mental health problems. I very clearly stated that I feared for his safety and his well-being if he were to be held overnight. Still, they would not release him.

I thought that sitting in a courthouse waiting to bail my baby boy out of jail was the low point in my life as a mom, but that wasn't the worst of it. Once we got him out and safely in our arms, I watched in horror as my son completely melted down. I'm not sure I have ever felt so helpless as I did in those moments of attempting to drive him home while he bawled and screamed in the back seat of our car. I was terrified he might try to throw himself into traffic, or do something else to hurt himself, and so we got off the highway and headed to the nearest hospital. He was triaged and assessed by their mental health team, and after much pleading and negotiation, they released him into our care rather than admitting him.

That was the start of a two-year journey down a road I never thought we would travel. While Tom was under house arrest, we all struggled to adjust to the new normal. We had many sleepless nights and nights where he pleaded with us to stay with him, to pray over him so he could have peace enough to sleep. He was devastated by what had happened the night of his arrest and could not come to terms with what that meant for his future. The medications were, in my opinion, making him worse before they would make him better. My fun-loving, happy-go-lucky boy with the quick wit and a sharp sense of humour was gone.

It is Well

He had been replaced by someone who was volatile, angry, confused, impulsive, and so deeply wounded, it was heartbreaking to witness. When I looked into his eyes, he just wasn't there. I despaired so much in those days, praying for God to preserve my son's life, and for Him to restore my baby to me.

There were a lot of dark days in the first few months after Tom's arrest. I felt like every other day, I was calling on the pastor, and asking him to pray, or to come over to help us in a clinch. I did not share our crisis with the church body at large because I felt that this was Tom's story to tell, and I didn't feel right in telling everyone what had happened to him. So, we kept it to ourselves, with only a few people at church knowing all the details.

I reached out to my family asking for prayer, and I asked the ladies of my home church in Ottawa to pray as well. The thing is, when I lived in Ottawa and Cayla was a baby, I would go to ladies' prayer meeting. Every Tuesday in the morning. I would walk into that prayer room, and immediately Cayla would be

It is Well

whisked from my arms and rocked while whoever held her prayed. That prayer room was a place where I felt safe, surrounded, and cocooned in love. It was also a place where we had seen the power of God move in the most miraculous of ways, and I knew that even if the ladies did not know what they were praying for, that they would take on this need in all earnestness.

One of the ladies from my home church reached out to me by phone. She said, "Every chance you get, go into your son's room. Pray over EVERYTHING. His bed, his pillow, his books, his phone, his clothes, his shoes, his computer. *Pray over everything.* Pray for the protection of God in his life. Pray for God's will to be done. Pray for the restoration of his mental health." I followed that advice to the letter then, and I still haven't stopped.

Just as the crisis was ramping up, I had to be away to speak at a church for their annual weekend seminar. God had been preparing my heart for this weekend for over a year, and the final message He impressed on me was called, "Choices, Choices" (see the final chapter in this book). The question was, "Do you trust in God, or don't you? Do you believe His Word, or don't you?" Little did I know that my life and that of our family would be in complete upheaval by the time I had to deliver this message. The day I was to preach this message, I felt the need to go to church in the morning. I went to my home church and just worshipped the Lord with all I had.

On returning to my hotel, I started receiving a flurry of texts from my son, desperate and distraught. He was threatening to end his life, saying he just couldn't take any more of the emotional pain. What could I do? I was more than 5 hours away by car. I couldn't get to him. I did what I could to get through to him via text, but in the end, I just begged him to seek out his dad, and to consider going to church that evening. Then I had no choice but to prepare myself for the afternoon service, but before I left my hotel room, I cried out to God one more time, and begged him to preserve Tom's life, and that he would change his mind and go to church.

It is Well

When I got up to speak, the weight of the burden I was carrying for my son was so heavy, I could hardly speak. Still, the message was delivered, and I believe God had laid that word on my heart for me, as much as for anyone else. Shortly after we got out of service, I received a text from my husband letting me know that Tom had decided to go to church with him. All I could do was praise God for keeping my baby safe.

The lowest point
About a month and a half after the arrest, Tom found out that he would not be allowed to return to school – it was such a hard blow to his self-esteem, he spiraled downward even further. It meant no more college – he had to withdraw from his post-secondary studies. That was absolutely shattering for him. It seemed that no amount of intervention would be able to stop him from spinning completely out of control – destroying things that were of value to him and hurting himself. Finally, after several visits from the police and mental health workers, he agreed to try to work with us so that he would not be breached, and he

would be able to stay at home. He was so angry, and furthermore, he felt betrayed that we had called the police in to intervene, that while he stopped acting out, he also stopped communicating with us. Every day, I would go into his room to bring him his medication and a glass of water and every day for over a month, the only two words he spoke to me were, "GET OUT."

Moms, can you feel the depth of that cut? This was my baby. The little one who almost died at birth, my miracle child. The stinker who was always up to something, cracking jokes, making me laugh, and giving me hugs. That boy was gone, and he had been replaced with an angry man who couldn't stand the sight of his own mother.

I cannot begin to tell you how much that hurt. How much time I spent on my knees with my husband and on my own, begging God to intervene. I wept and cried more in those few months than I had in years.

It is Well

In the middle of all of this, I had to keep it together to go to work. As someone who is self-employed, I just couldn't stop working indefinitely to see to this crisis. I went to work and kept getting new referrals. Every other new client was a mom about my age, with a son about Tom's age, who was going through something very similar to my challenge. I remember, holding one mom in my arms as she wept and whispering to her over and over, "It's not your fault," all the while thinking to myself, "How can I convince her of this, when I'm not sure that Tom's problems are not my fault?"

For a while I was mired in self-blame. I had attempted the Mom Blunder of doing it myself, and I had failed. I was sheathed in a cloak of mom-guilt and mom-shame, and I felt completely useless as a mother and as a therapist. I couldn't reconcile how I could possibly be a good therapist and not be able to help my own son. It was devastating to be drowning in such feelings of inadequacy and failure.

It is Well

In fact, there were days that I simply could not go to work. I couldn't sit in my office and tell another mom that she could trust in the process when I was having difficulty doing the same thing. I wasn't sure I would be able to make it through the day without breaking down into tears and losing my mind.

Then in the throes of all that drama, I was hired to go to Winnipeg for three days to do training. Tom was still giving me the silent treatment, but I knew the medication was finally working as it should. He stayed sequestered in his room all day, but he came out every day to shower and to get some food. I would slip into his room as soon as he made it into the shower, and I would pray over everything. I dreaded going away, but my husband and I agreed that perhaps the time away would be good for both Tom and me. Before I left, I said to him, "I really miss the days that we could just talk to each other." I expected no reply, but I felt I needed to let him know how much I missed our easy rapport.

It is Well

When I returned from Winnipeg, it had been about a month since he had stopped speaking to me. By that time, some of his bail conditions had been loosened, so he could go out with his brother, and to resume some of his activities. He came in from being out and saw me on the couch, and said, "Hey momma." In that moment, I felt like a little bit of hope that my boy was still in there.

The following eighteen months were still full of ups and downs. It took several months before the case against him was resolved. We encouraged him to go to therapy, and he continued with the medications until the doctor felt he could be weaned off them. We started to see glimmers of our boy breaking through the fog of medications and the depression they were treating. Little by little he returned to us.

Now, four years later, Tom is working full time, and pursuing the goals of most young men his age. He is learning to "adult" and carving out a career and a future for himself. More important than that, he is *alive*. His sense of humour has returned. Every now and then, he has a bad day, but the good days outweigh the bad. He hugs me every day. We can sit and talk about just about anything, just like we used to before things went horribly wrong. I still pray for the day that my boy, who is God-conscious will once again be God-committed and that his testimony will also be one of complete victory.

What got me through

As I said in the introduction, while we were in the throes of this 2-year long drama, I did not have time or the presence of mind to do any in-depth Bible study. I read the Psalms. I prayed the Psalms. I leaned heavily on my sisters and church family who were supporting me in prayer, and then I prayed the Psalms some more. Most of the scriptures that kept me have already been mentioned in the pages of this book, but one of the key ones was Proverbs 3:5-6. "Trust in the Lord with all thine heart." Every time I prayed to God, I reminded Him, "God, this is YOUR baby. You lent him to me, but I returned him to you that day I dedicated him and his brother in 1994.

He is Yours. I am trusting You to keep him safe. I don't know what else to do."

I knew in my heart that if I didn't take care, I could easily become bitter because of what had happened. Some things happened at church while I was at home seeing to my son that could have caused me to be angry, but when I looked at things objectively, I realized people couldn't be faulted for what they didn't know. I reached out to people in ministry that I thought would understand and help me pray, and I watched them retreat into themselves even as I poured out my heart to them. I realized then that not everyone in ministry is equipped to help people through a crisis.

Fear was my greatest enemy, and sometimes it still wars with my psyche. I recall the crippling, debilitating fear that I felt every time my son left the house. I feared for his safety more than anything, but to be honest, I was fearful all the time. When I woke up in the middle of the night and saw that he had not yet come home from spending time with

It is Well

his friends, I wouldn't be able to get back to sleep. I would "sleep with one eye open" so I could watch for his safe return. I understand that verse in Psalm 23 that discusses the "valley of the shadow of death". The shadow of death loomed over me constantly. Learning to trust in God to the point of overcoming fear; remembering that the perfect love of God casts out fear; and reminding myself that God has not given me the spirit of fear is how I managed then and now.

The real lesson for me was in trusting God. Through the pain. Through the fear. Through the heartbreak. Through the waiting. Through the land of in-between. Through the sleepless nights. Through the valley of the shadow of death. Through the nights of praying and sleeping in my son's room until he finally fell asleep.

I knew that If I just trusted in God, I could make it. I know on the surface that doesn't make sense, but that is the essence of faith, is it not? I had to ask myself, "Do I trust God's Word to be true or not?"

It is Well

One of the songs that kept me through this time was performed by Mercy Me and it is titled, "Even If". The chorus declares,

> "I know You're able
> And I know You can
> Save through the fire
> With Your mighty hand
> But even if You don't
> My hope is you alone.
> I know the sorrow
> And I know the hurt
> Will all go away
> If You just say the word
> But even if You don't
> My hope is You alone."[viii]

Like Shannon and Valerie, I did not want to look back on this awful time in my life and repent because I did not trust God enough. Like Abraham, I leaned on my staff, and remembered the times before that God had

It is Well

proved himself faithful, and I reminded myself over and over that God is the same yesterday, today, and forever. If He was faithful to us in the past, He would be faithful in this trial as well.

Again, like Valerie, I did not want this trial to be our ending. Most of all, I wanted this trial to become a testimony. I have always been of the mind that everything happens for a reason. Many times, throughout our crisis, I asked myself, "What's good about this?" Even if the answer was that "My boy is still alive. He's still here", it was enough. Through every hill and valley, I asked, "What can we learn from this?" "How will this help me be a better therapist?" "How can I use this crisis in future to minister to others who are in pain?" I believe with all my heart that staying focused on what God had in store for me and my family rather than the fire we were walking through helped me to savour the bitter, to become better, and finally to receive the blessing God had in store for me.

17
CHOICES, CHOICES

When God created man and breathed into his clay-formed frame the breath of life, He instilled within man the gift and the power of choice. He wants mankind to be in relationship with Him, but He wants us to enter that relationship willingly and with open hearts. He did not create us to be like the angels who can only do what they were created to do – nothing more, and nothing less. We are gifted with the ability to choose.

Every day we make choices – from the moment we wake, until the minute we retire for the night. We choose when to get out of bed, whether to make the bed, what to wear, how to wear our hair, what to eat, whether we will go to school or work. We choose to pray, to watch television, to read books, to play games. We choose to while away the hours watching cat videos on social media. We choose whether we will attend church or work in the kingdom of God. Every conscious thought, every decision, every action we take is a choice.

Two types of choices or decisions
In life, we have two types of choices: the choices that strengthen us, and the choices that weaken us. Eating that chocolate bar may taste good in the moment, but it is a weakening decision. Going for a walk to burn off stress and improve your cardio is a strengthening decision. Wallowing in self-pity and self-blame is a weakening decision. Turning your eyes towards heaven and placing your hope and trust in God is a strengthening decision.

Even in this, you have a choice. You can choose how to respond. You can choose the words you will say, and the timing of your responses. You can choose to pray and draw nearer to God, or you can choose to believe that He doesn't care about you, and that you have no option but to try and fix it yourself.

As a mom in a time of crisis, you will always have choices. You can choose to become mired in bitterness, fumbling around lost in the dark, tripping over Mom Blunders, or you can choose to turn the lights on, go through the process of self-evaluation, and seek out God's plan for your life through this fiery trial.

Do you, or don't you? The ultimate choice
I fear that the reasons so many of our churches are not seeing God move the way we want is because we are not fully believing that God can do it. Do we believe that God can heal? Do we believe He can deliver? Do we believe He will provide? Do we believe He can do it for US?

Consider the choices made by the prodigal son (Luke 15 v 11-24). A certain man had two sons: and the younger of them said to his father, "Father, give me the portion of goods that falleth to me". And he divided unto them his living.

It is Well

And not many days after the younger son gathered all together, and took his journey into a far country, and there wasted his substance with riotous living. And when he had spent all, there arose a mighty famine in that land; and he began to be in want. And he went and joined himself to a citizen of that country; and he sent him into his fields to feed swine. And he would fain have filled his belly with the husks that the swine did eat: and no man gave unto him.

And when he came to himself, he said, "How many hired servants of my father's have bread enough and to spare, and I perish with hunger! I will arise and go to my father, and will say unto him, 'Father, I have sinned against heaven, and before thee, and am no more worthy to be called thy son: make me as one of thy hired servants.'"

And he arose and came to his father. But when he was yet a great way off, his father saw him, and had compassion, and ran, and fell on his neck, and kissed him. And the son said unto him, "Father, I have sinned against heaven, and in thy sight, and am no more worthy to be called thy son."

But the father said to his servants, "Bring forth the best robe, and put it on him; and put a ring on his hand, and shoes on his feet: and bring hither the fatted calf, and kill it; and let us eat, and be merry: for this my son was dead, and is alive again; he was lost, and is found."

This boy chose to leave the safety and security of his father's home. He requested his inheritance, basically telling his father, "I'm not interested in waiting for you to die – I want my money now," and took his birthright to go his own way. His choices resulted in him ending up essentially on skid row – no money, no friends, no home, no prospects, defiling his body, his heritage and his religion.

He came to himself at his lowest point and made another choice – to return, to apologize, and to serve. Note that he had some faith in his father's love, and that faith was enough to spur him on toward home. His father also had a choice! He could have rejected his son, and he would have been within his rights to do so. Instead, he chose to forgive him, to love him, and to restore him to the family.

Now compare the above story with that of the "Good Samaritan" (Luke 10 v 30-37). "A certain man went down from Jerusalem to Jericho, and fell among thieves, which stripped him of his raiment, and wounded him, and departed, leaving him half dead. And by chance there came down a certain priest that way: and when he saw him, he passed by on the other side. And likewise, a Levite, when he was at the place, came and looked on him, and passed by on the other side.

But a certain Samaritan, as he journeyed, came where he was: and when he saw him, he had compassion on him, and went to him, and bound up his wounds, pouring in oil and wine, and set him on his own beast, and brought him to an inn, and took care of him. And on the morrow when he departed, he took out two pence, and gave them to the host, and said unto him, 'Take care of him; and whatsoever thou spendest more, when I come again, I will repay thee.'

The businessman chose a road that was meant to lead him to profit; however, the road he chose was a dangerous one. He may have known it was a dangerous road, but it may also have been the only route that would have taken him to his destination. It was not his choice to be attacked, robbed, or nearly killed; however, these things happened as a result of his choice.

The religious leaders who abandoned him to his fate also made a choice... they may have done so believing that they were justified because of their religion, their doctrines, or the law – but their choices also had consequence.

The Samaritan chose to have compassion and to help the man in need – even though the businessman would not have done the same for him because of his heritage.

It is Well

What we can learn from these stories:
1. Sometimes the choices we make land us in a heap of trouble. Sometimes we find trouble because of our own willful disobedience and rebellion, but sometimes it is just life happening.
2. Even in your lowest state, God sees you and will reach out for you if you cry out to him. He is standing there in the distance, waiting for you to choose Him – he is ready to rescue, to restore, to heal, and to forgive.
3. Every day our lives are made up of one choice after another – there are strengthening choices and weakening choices. The prodigal made both – he was weak in leaving; strong in returning. The businessman and the religious leaders made weakening choices; the Samaritan made strengthening ones that strengthened him as well as the man he saved.
4. Church leaders have a responsibility and an obligation to show compassion and care for those around them. In the Bible Study, "Big Ideas" by Bro. David

Norris presents the notion that there are only TWO types of people: those in covenant with God and those whom God is calling into covenant relationship. It is the responsibility of the church to CHOOSE to reach out to those whom God is calling into covenant relationship. When those of our flock are hurting – especially the "hard-to-serve", the "difficult-to-love" members of our assembly – it is even more incumbent upon us to reach out and to do as Jesus would have done. He commands us to "Go and do likewise" as the Good Samaritan did. Hard as it may be to choose to take up that mantle, that is what it means to be the hands and feet of Jesus.

The most important choice we can make is believing that God is, and that He will reward those who diligently seek him. When we really believe and truly trust in God, there is such strength and peace that comes with that decision because we can rest in Him. That doesn't mean we aren't going to cry sometimes. It doesn't mean that when life comes down on you HARD that you won't be battered and bruised within an inch of your life. What it DOES mean is that when you truly trust God you will have an ANCHOR that keeps your soul, steadfast and sure while the billows roll[ix].

You can choose to be in relationship, and you can choose how close you want that relationship to be. But I'll tell you right now, it is extremely difficult to trust someone you don't know well, and it is impossible to trust someone with whom you have no relationship. You can choose to push through the bitterness of your situation and allow God's grace to see you through and make you better. You can choose to trust God to be your strength despite what the world tries to throw at you. You can choose to "put on the whole armour of God", pressing forward with the shield of faith until you bash and discombobulate your enemy. You can choose to study the Word so you can wield the sword of the Spirit with deadly accuracy. You can

It is Well

choose to remain faithful in trusting God until He blesses you beyond measure.

You can choose.

Trust God enough to take hold of His promises even when what you see flies in the face of your faith:
- When your child calls you from the police station and says, "I'm in trouble"
- When your only son goes missing for months on end because of his addictive lifestyle
- When that backslidden loved one for whom you've been claiming the promises of God takes his/her own life
- When you lose your job and you can no longer support your family
- When your alcoholic mother abandons you when you need her most
- When your daughter is violated
- When your child is in a life-threatening accident
- When your child's mental health is precarious

- When your baby is born with a life-threatening illness

When everything goes wrong, **can you trust Him?** Will you trust Him?

Ask yourself if you can trust God even in the storm. Think of Jairus whose daughter lay dying and he cried out, "Lord I believe! Help thou mine unbelief!" (John 9 v 24). Isn't that how most of us feel in those rough moments?

Do you believe God is able even when He says NO? Can you still trust Him to take care of you even if He doesn't do what you want Him to do?

Listen up my sister. Trusting God is a strengthening decision – every time. Look through the stories in the Bible: Noah, Job, Joseph, Moses, Rahab, Ruth, Esther, David, Daniel, Shadrach, Meschach, & Abednego, Elijah, Elisha, Jonah, and others; the apostles and the prophets… trusting God worked in their favour EVERY TIME. Did that mean things always worked out the way they wanted? NO. But God was faithful – He IS faithful!

Cortt Chavis said, "A 'But if Not' attitude is the greatest attitude a Christian can have. I KNOW what God can do and what I want God to do, but if NOT, if He doesn't do it, I will still praise Him. I will still be here. I want/I need God to do something but if not, I will still love Him. I will still believe in Him. I will still trust Him. I will still be there on Sunday and I'll still worship Him."[x]

Christine Caine writes, "Today I challenge you to believe: There is no:
- Problem He cannot solve
- No question He cannot answer
- No disease He cannot heal
- No demon He cannot cast out
- No enemy He cannot overcome
- No bondage He cannot break
- No need He cannot meet
- And No mountain He cannot move[xi]

When tragedy strikes, we can choose to trust God and let Him turn our trials into our testimonies. Let's not be bitter like Job's wife or lose sight of where our hope lies like Elijah's angry widow. I pray we will daily surrender our children to the Lord and be like the Shunamite woman who was steadfast and faithful, showed grace under pressure and despite what her feelings told her amid tragedy, was able to say, "IT IS WELL".

It is Well

REFERENCES AND PERMISSIONS

[i] Kenyon, J. (2018). What is the Strongest and Hardest Metals Known to Man? *Owlcation.com*. Retrieved from https://owlcation.com/stem/What-is-the-Strongest-Metal-The-Hardest-Metals-Known-to-Man

[ii] Bradberry, T. (2016). Complaining rewires your brain for negativity. Published on *Entrepreneur.com*, and updated April 10, 2017 for *The Globe and Mail*. Retrieved from https://www.theglobeandmail.com/report-on-business/small-business/sb-growth/how-complaining-rewires-your-brain-for-negativity/article31893948/

[iii] Ritenbaugh, R.T. (1999). Elisha and the Shumanite Woman, Part II: Serving God's Children. *Forerunner*. October 1999 Issue. Retrieved from https://www.cgg.org/index.cfm/fuseaction/Library.sr/CT/ARTB/k/145/Elisha-and-Shunammite-Woman-Part-II-Serving-Gods-Chidren.htm

[iv] Historium.com. Using a Shield for Offensive Attack. Retrieved from https://historum.com/threads/using-a-shield-for-offensive-attack.73949/

It is Well

[v] Youtube video of the Provocatori: "Ars Dimicandi – Galli a Riolo Terme 2009". Retrieved from https://www.youtube.com/watch?v=a41zapoBhIM
[vi] Definition of FAITH – *Webster's Dictionary for Everyday Use*. (1986). Miami: PSI & Associates, Inc.
[vii] Definition of TRUST – *Webster's Dictionary*. (1986).
[viii] MercyMe, David Garcia, Ben Glover, Crystal Lewis, Tim Timmons, (2016). Even If. *"Lifer"*. Released by Fair Trade/Columbia Records.
[ix] Priscilla J Owens and William J Kirkpatrick. (n.d.) We Have an Anchor. *Sing Unto the Lord*, pub. 1978. Hazelwood: Word Aflame Press.
[x] Social media meme – Facebook.com
[xi] Social media meme – Facebook.com

Scripture quotations are from the King James Version of the Bible. Copyright (c) 1973 by Word Aflame Press.

Shannon Milton's story and testimony used with permission.

Camilla and Valerie's story used with permission.

Julie and Tom's story used with permission.

Scripture quotations from the North American Standard Version of the Holy Bible, YouVersion Bible App.

It is Well

Scripture quotations from the King James Version of the Holy Bible, retrieved from Theophilos for Windows, Version 3.1.6, ©1997-2004.

Acknowledgements

Writing a book this personal is never an easy process. I would not have been able to do it without the support of my friends and family. I want to extend my thanks and gratitude to Camilla and Valerie*, Shannon and Braidyn Milton, and my son Thomas for allowing me to share your very personal, and in some cases, your most private experiences. I truly believe that God will use your testimonies to bless people in ways we cannot even begin to imagine.

I'd like to extend my thanks to Sonia Senior-Martin for being my friend, my sister in Christ and in love, and for applying her incredible grasp of the English language to the editing and proofreading of this manuscript.

Thank you to the ladies of my home church, Calvary Church in Ottawa, Ontario, who held me up in prayer and shared words of encouragement that were always on point, even though you knew nothing of our situation. Thanks also to my pastor and bishop of New Life Church Niagara, who stepped in with moral support, physical interventions, and prayer whenever we needed it.

I must also acknowledge my family for their prayerful support, especially my sister, Kathy who stepped up to be an emotional support when I needed her.

I'd like to also acknowledge Sister Janice Sjostrand for hearing God's voice and for being obedient in sharing His heart.

I must acknowledge my husband Stevan who stood by our boy from start to finish of our crisis, and who tolerates the mental fugue that ensues whenever I become immersed in writing. I promise to respond to your conversation points with more than "Hmmm" from now on!

Lastly, none of this would have been possible without the divine intervention of my Lord and Saviour, Jesus Christ. He is my everything, my all-in-all, and I am forever

It is Well

grateful that He calls me His child and that He watches over my family. It is because of Him that I am so BLESSED.